M000305642

A LEADER'S GUIDE TO COMPETENCY-BASED EDUCATION

A LEADER'S GUIDE TO COMPETENCY-BASED EDUCATION

From Inception to Implementation

Deborah J. Bushway, Laurie Dodge, and Charla S. Long

Foreword by Amy Laitinen

STERLING, VIRGINIA

COPYRIGHT © 2018 BY
STYLUS PUBLISHING, LLC.

Published by Stylus Publishing, LLC.
22883 Quicksilver Drive
Sterling, Virginia 20166-2019

All rights reserved. No part of this book may be reprinted
or reproduced in any form or by any electronic, mechanical,
or other means, now known or hereafter invented, including
photocopying, recording, and information storage and
retrieval, without permission in writing from the publisher.

Library of Congress Cataloging-in-Publication Data
Names: Bushway, Deborah J., author. | Dodge, Laurie Graham,
author. | Long, Charla S., author.
Title: A leader's guide to competency-based education : from
inception to implementation / Deborah J. Bushway, Laurie Dodge,
& Charla S. Long.
Description: First edition. |
Sterling, Virginia : Stylus Publishing, LLC, [2018] |
Includes bibliographical references and index.
Identifiers: LCCN 2017038996 (print) |
LCCN 2017060174 (ebook) |
ISBN 9781620365953 (ePub, mobi) |
ISBN 9781620365946 (uPDF) |
ISBN 9781620365922 (cloth : acid-free paper) |
ISBN 9781620365939 (paperback. : acid-free paper) |
ISBN 9781620365946 (library networkable e-edition) |
ISBN 9781620365953 (consumer e-edition)
Subjects: LCSH: Competency-based education--Handbooks,
manuals, etc.
Classification: LCC LC1031 (ebook) |
LCC LC1031 .B87 2018 (print) |
DDC 370.11--dc23
LC record available at https://lccn.loc.gov/2017038996

13-digit ISBN: 978-1-62036-592-2 (cloth)
13-digit ISBN: 978-1-62036-593-9 (paperback)
13-digit ISBN: 978-1-62036-594-6 (library networkable e-edition)
13-digit ISBN: 978-1-62036-595-3 (consumer e-edition)

Printed in the United States of America

All first editions printed on acid-free paper
that meets the American National Standards Institute
Z39-48 Standard.

Bulk Purchases

Quantity discounts are available for use in workshops and for
staff development.
Call 1-800-232-0223

First Edition, 2018

CONTENTS

Foreword

Competency-based education (CBE) is having its moment in the sun. Although CBE has been around on a relatively small scale for decades, over the past five years we have seen CBE go from a relatively obscure model of higher education to one that President Obama called out in a State of the Union address. We have gone from a handful of schools operating CBE programs to over 600 colleges actively exploring creating such programs. Members of Congress, the U.S. Department of Education, governors, state legislatures, chancellors, and college presidents are all now talking about CBE. That's the good news.

The bad news is there hasn't been an agreed-on definition of *CBE*. Early in this book the authors say, "If you were to ask 10 people to define *CBE* you would likely hear 10 different answers" (p. 2, this volume). I disagree. I think it's likely you would get at least 15 different answers. To call this a challenge—for policymakers, for practitioners, for students, for employers—would significantly understate the problem. Without agreed-on terms and practices, there is significant danger of *CBE* becoming meaningless, an empty term onto which policymakers at all levels can project their higher education fantasies.

The most common fantasy I hear around CBE is that it will be cheaper, faster, and better. Maybe it will be all of these things or maybe it won't be any. Before knowing if CBE will be better than what we have, we'd have to have a sense of what the quality of traditional higher education is. And we don't. The promise of a well-designed CBE program is that it will provide transparency about both the learning expectations and outcomes. That level of transparency is shockingly lacking in traditional higher education. CBE sounds great in theory, but how does one go about creating a high-quality CBE program?

Much to the chagrin of those of us who would like quick and easy fixes, moving to high-quality CBE is neither. Making it happen requires rolling up one's sleeves and doing the deep, difficult, time-consuming work necessary to create an intentional, sustainable, high-quality CBE culture and program. There are no shortcuts. The task requires asking tough questions all along the way and the courage to admit when something is not working. The authors of this book have done the hard work of grappling with questions around program design, assessment, supporting students through their learning journey, faculty and staffing models, business models, processes, and systems, and internal and external approvals. And they are sharing their lessons learned—sometimes painfully learned—with us.

This book is invaluable for anyone looking to start, or examine, their own CBE program. There are no better guides than these three leading-edge practitioners. Deborah J. Bushway, Laurie Dodge, and Charla S. Long are practitioners who have created their own programs and have worked with institutions from all over the country to help them build not just their own high-quality CBE programs but a high-quality CBE movement. Happy reading!

Amy Laitinen
Director of Higher Education
New America | Education Policy Program

INTRODUCTION

Over the past few years, higher education in the United States has seen an increase in interest in competency-based education (CBE). In a recent survey, 97% of institutions surveyed say they are at least interested in CBE (Garrett & Lurie, 2016). Yet, there are relatively few schools that have been able to move from interest to implementation. This book is designed to help institutional leaders become more competent in designing, building, and scaling high-quality CBE programs. In this introduction, we will

- define *competency-based education*;
- provide an overview of the history of the movement, including the current resurgence; and
- describe the current state of the movement.

What Is CBE?

Before we define *CBE*, it is best to start by clarifying what is meant by a *competency*. A competency is the capability to apply or use a set of related knowledge, skills, abilities, and intellectual behaviors required to successfully perform tasks in a defined setting (see Figure I.1).

When determining the competencies that will compose an academic program, we focus on what is needed for the credential

Figure I.1. Graphic representation of a competency.

Knowledge	Skills & Abilities	Intellectual Behaviors	Application & Transfer
What does the learner need to know?	What does the learner need to be able to do?	What dispositions does the learner need to display?	Where will the learner apply these competencies and at what level?

1

or degree holder to be successful. At the point of credential completion, the learner should know the theory of his or her discipline
and have the skills, abilities, and dispositions to successfully apply
the theory in the desired setting.

If you were to ask 10 people to define *CBE*, you would likely
hear 10 different answers, as there is no universal or regulatory
definition of the term. An often-cited definition, crafted by
the Competency-Based Education Network (2015), stated the
following:

> Competency-based education combines an intentional and
> transparent approach to curricular design with an academic
> model in which the time it takes to demonstrate competen-
> cies varies and the expectations about learning are held con-
> stant. Students acquire and demonstrate their knowledge and
> skills by engaging in learning exercises, activities and experi-
> ences that align with clearly defined programmatic outcomes.
> Students receive proactive guidance and support from faculty
> and staff. Learners earn credentials by demonstrating mastery
> through multiple forms of assessment, often at a personalized
> pace. (para. 1)

The Council of Regional Accrediting Commissions (2015)
defined *CBE* as

> an outcomes-based approach to earning a college degree
> or other credential. Competencies are statements of what
> students can do as a result of their learning at an institu-
> tion of higher education. While competencies can include
> knowledge or understanding, they primarily emphasize what
> students can do with their knowledge. Students progress
> through degree or credential programs by demonstrating
> competencies specified at the course and/or program level.
> The curriculum is structured around these specified com-
> petencies, and satisfactory academic progress is expressed as
> the attainment or mastery of the identified competencies.
> Because competencies are often anchored to external expec-
> tations, such as those of employers, to pass a competency stu-
> dents must generally perform at a level considered to be very
> good or excellent. (p. 2)

Regardless of the origin of the *CBE* definition, there are several hallmarks of competency-based programs.

Time Is Variable, and Learning Is Fixed

Today's higher education model confines learning to set periods of time, such as a 15-week term, and achievement of credentials by the number of credit hours accumulated, typically 60 credits for an associate's degree and 120 credits for a bachelor's degree. Throughout and at the conclusion of a fixed period of time, learning is assessed, and a student is measured by what he or she knows. A student may know only 60% to 70% of the material and would still get credit for the course, whereas another student may achieve 80% to 100% of the course material. Although the learning varied for these students, they each received credit for the course. This is known as making time fixed and learning variable.

In CBE programs, this is switched. Learning becomes fixed, while the time it takes to master learning varies. Learners are provided with a program's set of competencies that they must know and be able to demonstrate in order to earn the credential—period. This learning is held constant and is nonnegotiable. The learner can go as fast as or as slowly as is needed because time is not confining the learning process.

Required Demonstration of Mastery or Proficiency

In CBE programs, each competency must be mastered before the learner can earn the credential. Some institutions use proficiency-based language, saying a student must become proficient in the competency before graduation. Regardless of the language used, the result is the same: A learner cannot hide the lack of competence in one area by performing well in another and earning an overall passing grade. Each and every competency must be learned and demonstrated before learners successfully complete the program.

Determined by Rigorous Assessments

To determine if a student has mastered a competency, an institution must use rigorous assessments. If an institution is going to prohibit a learner from graduating because of the lack of competence, the institution's assessment tools must be proven as reliable and valid indicators of mastery of learning in each competency. Because of the essential nature of assessment, an entire chapter of this book focuses on how to design a robust assessment strategy for a CBE program.

Focused on the Student Learning Journey

CBE programs are committed to intentionally constructing a student learning journey that leads to the demonstration of mastery for each competency. Students are not left on their own to learn; rather, they are guided by faculty throughout their academic experience via learning activities, readings, and assignments designed to move them from current performance to the desired level of competency mastery. Learning is not left to chance. Rather, the entire learning journey is carefully crafted to ensure consistency and results.

Offered in a Flexible, Self-Paced Approach

Typically, CBE programs are designed to personalize a learner's academic experience by offering a flexible, self-paced approach. In CBE programs, institutions are diligent in building flexibility into the program's design. This allows students to set their own pace of learning, which means students have the opportunity to move quickly as they demonstrate competence and to go as slowly as they need to master more difficult content.

What Is the History of the CBE Movement?

Around the turn of the twentieth century, wealthy industrialist Andrew Carnegie wanted to honor college professors for their noble work by making $10 million available for retirement pensions through the Carnegie Foundation for the Advancement of Teaching (1906). The *Carnegie Unit* was created for multiple reasons, including as the standard unit for setting faculty-threshold measures that determined who qualified for pension payments. This unit was never intended to be the proxy for learning, as professors were left to determine if learning actually occurred. Yet, over time, the Carnegie Unit has often become the metric for determining if a student has earned a given credential.

Pioneer institutions in the CBE movement began in the 1970s. Alverno College's ability-based curriculum with its robust outcomes framework still serves as a model for institutions today. Institutions like Regents College (now Excelsior College), DePaul School of New Learning, Charter Oak State College, and Thomas Edison State University wanted to serve adult learners and looked for ways to grant college credit for learning that occurred outside of a typical classroom. Through prior learning assessment methods, these institutions used demonstrable outcomes to measure what a learner knew and could do and transferred these demonstrations into credits. Students with these credits experienced a more flexible completion pathway. Yet, other institutions did not broadly adopt these methods of measuring a learner's competencies, and the number of institutions affected remained confined to a small handful.

In 1995, U.S. governors from the Western Governors Association were discussing the higher education challenges in their respective states. Together, these governors envisioned a new kind of collaborative university, one that would utilize distance learning technology and use competencies as its measure of learning ("The Unique History of WGU," 2017). These governors signed on to create Western Governors University (WGU), which was established as a private, nonprofit university two years later. In 1999, WGU began accepting its first students, and in 2016, WGU enrolled over 76,000 students. Despite WGU's success, no other universities followed suit, and this iteration of CBE remained confined to this single institution.

When the Higher Education Reconciliation Act of 2005 (HERA) was being negotiated by the U.S. Congress, WGU advocated for the inclusion of a "direct assessment" provision in the bill. HERA modified the Higher Education Act of 1965 and allowed Title IV funds for programs that used, in lieu of credit hours or clock hours, the direct assessment of student learning. As defined, *direct assessment programs* measure what a student knows and can do in terms of the academic program and awards credentials and financial aid on this basis alone. An institution must receive the U.S. Department of Education's approval to use direct assessment, but, interestingly, WGU never sought this approval, and the direct assessment provision went unused for a number of years (see Figure I.2).

Figure I.2. Direct assessment programs.

Direct Assessment Programs

1. A direct assessment program is an instructional program that, in lieu of credit hours or clock hours as a measure of student learning, uses direct assessment of student learning or recognizes the direct assessment of student learning by others. The assessment must be consistent with the accreditation of the institution or program using the results of the assessment.

2. Direct assessment of student learning means a measure by the institution of what a student knows and can do in terms of the body of knowledge making up the educational program. These measures provide evidence that a student has command of a specific subject, content area, or skill or that the student demonstrates a specific quality such as creativity, analysis, or synthesis associated with the subject matter of the program. Examples of direct measures include projects, papers, examinations, presentations, performances, and portfolios.

3. All regulatory requirements in this chapter that refer to credit or clock hours as a measurement apply to direct assessment programs. Because a direct assessment program does not use credit or clock hours as a measure of student learning, an institution must establish a methodology to reasonably equate the direct assessment program (or the direct assessment portion of any program, as applicable) to credit or clock hours for the purpose of complying with applicable regulatory requirements. The institution must provide a factual basis satisfactory to the secretary for its claim that the program or portion of the program is equivalent to a specific number of credit or clock hours.

The direct assessment provision began to receive attention when Amy Laitinen (2012), New America Foundation, released her transformative report *Cracking the Credit Hour*. The report showed how the use of a credit-hour system as the sole measure of learning was jeopardizing the nation's workforce and causing the United States to fall further behind in the rankings of the most educated nations in the world. Laitinen argued that institutions, regulators, and accreditors needed to move from *paying for and valuing time* to *paying for and valuing learning*. To move away from time-based representations of learning, institutions had to create another form of currency. The demonstration of competencies, as a true measure of learning, was the proposed alternative learning "currency."

Immediately after the release of *Cracking the Credit Hour*, institutions around the country began working on the next generation of competency-based programs, leveraging advancements in learning technologies, improving on existing CBE models, and seeking to do this without being tethered to the credit or clock hours. Early in 2013, Southern New Hampshire University's College for America became the first institution approved to award federal financial aid based on direct assessment instead of the credit hour. That same year, Capella University and the University of Wisconsin–Extension received direct assessment approval. In the months and years that have followed, a handful of institutions submitted applications for the U.S. Department of Education's approval.

The leaders of these innovative institutions faced many barriers, often talking about how they worked in isolation and desired a place to work with others who shared a similar vision for CBE. In 2013, with funding support from the Lumina Foundation and managerial support from the Public Agenda Foundation, the Competency-Based Education Network (C-BEN) was formed to create a safe space for these institutions to work together to address shared challenges in designing, developing, and scaling competency-based degree programs. C-BEN has established its reputation for openly sharing lessons learned and helping to equip other higher education leaders with the tools and resources needed to be effective in building high-quality competency-based offerings.

Over the past few years and with support from then-president Barack Obama, as demonstrated by the inclusion of CBE in various higher education speeches, leaders from the U.S. Department of Education encouraged a spirit of innovation in postsecondary education, especially in regard to CBE. In a department-issued "Dear Colleague" letter in early 2013, the acting assistant secretary for postsecondary education wrote,

> Competency-based approaches to education have the potential for assuring the quality and extent of learning, shortening the time to degree/certificate completion, developing stackable credentials that ease student transitions between school and work, and reducing the overall cost of education for both career-technical and degree programs. The Department plans to collaborate with both accrediting agencies and the higher education community to encourage the use of this innovative approach when appropriate, to identify the most promising

practices in this arena, and to gather information to inform future policy regarding competency-based education. Currently, the direct assessment authority in the HEA is the mechanism through which Title IV, HEA funds can be provided for competency-based education, and we understand that it may not adequately accommodate this educational model. The Department intends to use what we learn from participating institutions to inform future discussions regarding the reauthorization of the HEA. (Bergeron, 2013, para. 7)

The department's First in the World grant program supported the development, replication, and dissemination of new models of learning such as CBE. The department, acting under the authority given to it by Congress in the Higher Education Act of 1965, established two different rounds of experimental sites related to CBE (see Figure I.3).

Figure I.3. U.S. Department of Education experimental sites related to CBE.

Prior Learning Assessment: Provides that a student's Title IV cost of attendance (COA) can include costs incurred by the student for assessments of prior learning and that a student's federal Pell Grant enrollment status may, with limitations, take into account a student's efforts to prepare materials for a prior learning assessment.

Competency-Based Education: Provides flexibility in how institutions provide federal student aid to students enrolled in self-paced competency-based education programs.

Limited Direct Assessment: Provides flexibility for an institution to provide a mix of direct assessment course work and credit- or clock-hour course work in the same program.

Expansion of Waivers: The expansion of the current competency-based education experiment provides two additional sets of statutory and regulatory waivers. Institutions must choose a single set of waivers from among the three sets available that will apply to all of the competency-based education programs that it includes under the experiment. These waivers are split disbursement, satisfactory academic progress only, or subscription period disbursement.

Note. From Federal Student Aid (2017, December 14). See https://experimentalsites.ed .gov/exp/approved.html for more information.

For applying schools that were accepted into the experiment, the secretary of education granted waivers from certain Title IV, HEA statutory, or regulatory requirements to allow this limited number of institutions to participate in experiments to test alternative methods for awarding aid. The results from these experiments are not known at the time of this publication (see Table I.1).

Even though the U.S. Department of Education signaled to institutions its support for CBE, the department's Office of Inspector General (OIG) has consistently given contrary signals. Over the course of a few years, the OIG has "dumped a bucket of cold water" on CBE innovation with four significant investigative reports, summarized in Table I.2. Each report seemed to slow the progress being made by institutions, but most forged ahead with a commitment to innovate responsibly.

TABLE I.1
Must Reads From the Department of Education on CBE

Title	Date Issued	Relevance
Applying for Title IV Eligibility for Direct Assessment (Competency-Based) Programs (See https://ifap.ed.gov/dpcletters/GEN1310.html)	March 19, 2013	Describes direct assessment programs and outlines the process for receiving department approval.
Competency-Based Education Programs—Questions and Answers (See https://ifap.ed.gov/dpcletters/GEN1423.html)	December 19, 2014	Clarifies the March 19, 2013, "Dear Colleague"(Bergeron, 2013) letter.
Letter to Accrediting Agency Executive Directors (See www.insidehighered.com/sites/default/server_files/files/ED%20letter%20to%20accreditors(1).pdf)	June 9, 2015	Describes the roles and responsibilities of the accreditor and the department related to CBE experimental sites.

Note. CBE = competency-based education.

TABLE I.2

U.S. Department of Education Office of
Inspector General CBE-Related Reports

Title of Report	Date Issued	Relevance
Direct Assessment Programs: Processes for Identifying Risks and Evaluating Applications for Title IV Eligibility Needs Strengthening to Better Mitigate Risks Posed to the Title IV Programs (See www2.ed.gov/ about/offices/list/oig/ auditreports/fy2014/ a05n0004.pdf)	September 30, 2014	Determined the department had not adequately addressed the risks posed by direct assessment programs and had not established sufficient processes to ensure only programs meeting federal regulatory requirements are approved as Title IV eligible.
The Higher Learning Commission Could Improve Its Evaluation of Competency-Based Education Programs to Help the Department Ensure the Programs Are Properly Classified for Title IV Purposes (See www2.ed.gov/ about/offices/list/oig/ auditreports/fy2015/ a05o0010.pdf)	September 30, 2015	The Higher Learning Commission did not establish a system of internal control that provided reasonable assurance that schools' classification of delivery methods and measurements of student learning for CBE programs, including direct assessment, were sufficient and appropriate to help the department ensure that it properly classified the schools' programs for Title IV purposes.
The Western Association of Schools and Colleges [WASC] Senior College and University Commission Could Improve Its Evaluation of Competency-Based Education Programs to	August 2, 2016	WASC control activities did not provide reasonable assurance that schools properly classified the methods of delivery for CBE programs.

(*Continues*)

TABLE 1.2 (*Continued*)

Title of Report	Date Issued	Relevance
Help the Department Ensure Programs Are Properly Classified for Title IV Purposes (See www2.ed.gov/ about/offices/list/oig/ auditreports/fy2016/ a05p0013.pdf)		The commission did not evaluate whether proposed CBE programs were designed to ensure faculty-initiated, regular, and substantive interaction between faculty and students
Western Governors University Was Not Eligible to Participate in the Title IV Programs (See https://www 2.ed.gov/about/offices/ list/oig/auditreports/ fy2017/a05m0009.pdf)	September 20, 2017	The audit states WGU academic offerings are correspondence programs, making them ineligible to participate in Title IV programs. The Office of Inspector General concludes, based on distance learning requirements, that WGU programs lacked regular and substantive interaction between faculty and students. The audit proposes that WGU repay nearly $713 million in Title IV funds. The report does not specifically address CBE.

Note. CBE = competency-based education.

Regional and specialized accreditors have also been affected by the CBE movement. A lack of consistency between these quality-assurance entities caused confusion and challenges for institutions and prompted questions by regulators. When the Council of Regional Accrediting Commissions issued its joint definitional statement on CBE in June 2015, it shared a common framework to be used by regional accreditors when evaluating CBE programs (Council of Regional Accrediting Commissions, 2015) (see Figure I.4).

Figure I.4. Council of Regional Accrediting Commission's evaluation considerations for CBE programs.

1. Whether or not the institution demonstrates the capacity to offer competency-based or direct assessment programs, including administrative capacity and significant expertise in assessment that will ensure the reliability and validity of the assessments.
2. Whether or not most of the proposed learning outcomes emphasize performance, not simply knowledge.
3. Whether or not proposed competencies are externally referenced (e.g., referenced by convened groups of employers, professional advisory committees, or licensure requirements).
4. Whether or not the institution ensures "regular and substantive interaction" with faculty, as defined by the U.S. Department of Education, and appropriate services for students.
5. Whether or not the institution demonstrates that the competencies for a degree cohere to the claims that the institution makes for the qualifications of graduates, including at the undergraduate level those qualifications traditionally associated with general education and the major or concentration.
6. Whether or not the institution demonstrates that the level and complexity of the competencies are congruent with the achievement expected at a particular degree level (e.g., a competency in oral presentation skills for a BS in management is demonstrated at the baccalaureate level).
7. Whether or not the quality of demonstration of the competence is judged to be at or near the "excellent" range for each competency.
8. Whether or not a student must demonstrate each relevant competency in order to earn the degree or certificate.
9. Whether or not the institution follows good practices in assessment and measurement (e.g., determines reliability and validity and has multiple forms or prompts for each competency).
10. Whether or not a high proportion of the proposed competencies represent authentic demonstrations.
11. Whether or not the institution validates the quality of its program through feedback from students and graduates, as well as measures appropriate to the external reference of the competencies (e.g., licensure passage rates, earnings of graduates, feedback from employers who helped articulate the desired competencies).

Though institutions still struggle to understand regional accreditor requirements for CBE programs, this joint statement helped to reduce concerns about differing standards between these commissions.

Why Is CBE Experiencing a Resurgence?

Despite all of the challenges, institutions continue to push ahead in designing and launching competency-based offerings. College leaders have expressed a wide range of motivations for exploring CBE, including the many captured in the following sections.

Need for an Alternative to Today's Higher Education Model

For many learners, today's higher education model has not worked well. Many learners begin college but never complete their credential. A recent National Student Clearinghouse Research Center report found that just over half of all students (54.8%) complete a degree or certificate within six years (Shapiro et al., 2017). When the completers were examined by racial and ethnic lines, the percentage of completers varied up to 25%. Whites (62%) and Asians (63.2%) completed at higher rates than Hispanics (45.8%) or Blacks (38%). For students who began their postsecondary careers at community colleges, the likelihood of having a baccalaureate degree within six years of their start date was even worse. Asian (1 in 4) and White (1 in 5) students were most likely to complete this transfer pathway, whereas Hispanic (1 in 10) and Black (1 in 12) students were not. Today's model of higher education is clearly not serving all learners well. A high-quality alternative is needed, and CBE is one option (Shapiro et al., 2017).

The Iron Triangle: Cost, Access, and Quality

For years, three significant challenges facing higher education are how to reduce the costs of college, increase access to a greater number of learners from diverse backgrounds, and maintain or enhance the quality of the academic experience and outcomes. These three challenges, often collectively referred to as the *iron triangle*, need to be addressed simultaneously. In a small study of college presidents, many expressed a belief that two out of the three challenges could be met but not without negatively affecting the third (Immerwahr, Johnson, & Gasbarra, 2008). For example, it may be possible for a university to further drive down costs while increasing access to a new generation of learners, but most fear it would affect the quality of education received by learners. Many CBE programs seek, often inadvertently, to achieve all three dimensions of the iron triangle through streamlined processes, redesigned systems and structures, and a different business model. Future research is needed to determine if CBE programs can deliver on this promise to be high quality, with lower costs and greater access.

Desire To Be First in the World

The Organisation for Economic Co-operation and Development's (2014) *Education at a Glance* paints a less-than-optimistic picture of the U.S. higher education landscape. The United States ranks 14th in the world in the percentage of 25- to 34-year-olds with higher education (42%). For young people without college-educated parents, the likelihood of having higher education is just 29%, one of the lowest percentages among developed nations. In 2009, President Obama set a 2020 College Completion Goal that 60% of Americans ages 24 to 34 years would have an associate's or baccalaureate degree (Obama, 2009). To hit this goal, 10 million additional Americans (beyond the 8 million already anticipated enrollees) would need to enter the higher education system. There are many challenges inhibiting the United States from hitting this goal, including reductions in state funding for 4-year public institutions, a 439% increase in tuition in the past 35 years, and myriad other issues primarily associated with community colleges such as transfer practices, developmental education, and serving military veterans (Kanter, Ochoa, Nassif, & Chong, 2011).

The Lumina Foundation research shows that U.S. progress is not on track for hitting the 2020 goal set by then-president Obama or the foundation's goal of 60% of Americans earning a high-quality credential by 2025. As of 2015, the national average sits at 45.8%, with workforce-relevant certificates being included in this number. No state has reached the 60% attainment goal, although nine states have achieved over 50% (Lumina Foundation, 2017c). Because CBE recognizes that postsecondary learning can occur anywhere and creates pathways to postsecondary credentials for those otherwise not engaged in the current higher education system, the Lumina Foundation has invested heavily in competency-based learning as part of its Goal 2025 strategy (Lumina Foundation, 2017b).

Increase Graduate Preparedness

According to PayScale and Future Workplace, nearly 90% of all recent college graduates consider themselves well prepared for the workforce. Unfortunately, less than half of hiring managers agreed with their assessment. Sixty percent said new graduates lacked critical thinking skills and attention to details, 44% identified issues with written communication competencies, and 39% identified issues with oral communication competencies (PayScale and Future Workplace, 2016). The Educational Testing Service, using data from the Program for the International Assessment of Adult Competencies (PIAAC), found more than half of U.S. workers between the ages of 16 and 34 years lacked proficiency in reading and math skills in the workplace, which is on par with those in the least educated of participating countries in the survey (Goodman, Sands, & Coley, 2015). CBE focuses on the demonstration of learning and requires mastery before credential completion. This requirement should result in a more competent and prepared graduate, citizen, and worker.

Meet Future Workforce Needs

The percentage of jobs requiring postsecondary education has doubled over the past 40 years, and by 2020, two-thirds of all jobs will require a postsecondary education (Carnevale, Smith, & Strohl, 2013). Four out of five jobs lost during the last recession were those requiring a high school education or less, and these jobs are being replaced by those that require more complex knowledge, skills, and abilities—and a postsecondary credential (Lumina Foundation, 2017a). To help employees acquire the needed competencies, employers spend approximately $22 billon on college tuition reimbursement benefits, which represents over 5% of total spending on college and university tuition (Craig, 2016). In addition, employers spent nearly $71 billion on workforce-based training initiatives in 2015 alone. Small companies spent the most, at over $1,100 per employee, with large employers reaping the economies of scale and spending just under $450 per employee. The majority of training expenditures went to training nonexempt employees (39%) and exempt nonmanagers (29%) ("2015 Training Industry Report," 2015). High-quality CBE programs are designed with the needs of the workplace in mind. From incorporating twenty-first-century skills to creating customized programs to address a regional workforce shortage, CBE programs are able to respond more quickly to the needs of the workforce. In time, research will show whether CBE programs lead to a better prepared workforce.

Offer Personalized Learning

Higher education can learn a lesson from the K–12 sector on personalized learning. iNACOL defined *personalized learning* as "tailoring learning for each student's strengths, needs and interests—including enabling student voice and choice in what, how, when, and where they learn—to provide flexibility and supports to ensure mastery of the highest standards possible" (Abel, 2016, para. 4). Through the use of today's technology, the learning journey can be adapted to meet the individual student's needs. This means that learning experiences, instructional approaches, and support strategies should vary from learner to learner, based on the needs, interests, aspirations, and cultural backgrounds of individual students. By personalizing the learning journey, higher education keeps students the central focus during their postsecondary experience, which arguably increases the quality of the credential and the achievement of desired attainment rates. CBE programs seek to find ways to tailor the learning journey to the specific needs of each learner.

Adult Learners Are Demanding CBE

Although CBE programs can and do serve traditional-age students, the vast majority of CBE programs target adult learners. A 2013 Eduventures survey of over 7,500 adult learners revealed the desires of this student segment. The most requested needs were for more self-paced courses (42%) and a faster way to earn a degree (40%) (Fleming, 2014). Adult learners are looking for the very characteristics that define CBE programs. Learners want to remove time from the equation and proceed with their degree at their own pace. This means allowing students to go faster when they are capable and slower when they need more assistance or are balancing a heavier load in their personal and professional lives. The defining characteristics of CBE programs meet the needs of most adult learners in the United States today.

What Is the Current State of the Movement?

The CBE movement has benefited from a tremendous amount of coverage in the press over the past few years. Rarely does a week go by without a CBE story in *Inside Higher Ed* or *The Chronicle* highlighting an institutional model, a research report on a data set, or some advancement in the field. Yet, it was not always this way.

Just five years ago, institutions were building CBE programs in silos, often unaware of the innovative developments at other institutions. In 2012, the Lumina Foundation and the Bill and Melinda Gates Foundation cohosted a convening of 23 institutions operating or exploring the creation of a CBE program (C-BEN, 2015). One year later, the number had grown to nearly 200 (Hope, 2015). In 2015, with funding from the Bill and Melinda Gates Foundation, Public Agenda undertook the last count of the field and determined nearly 600 institutions were actively exploring the design and development of a CBE program (Fain, 2015a). A recent survey of nearly 200 college presidents found that nearly two-thirds are planning to offer some form of CBE by 2020 (Selingo, 2015).

Much has transpired since 2015, and the current state of the movement is not completely clear. Yet, despite this uncertainty, C-BEN is dedicated to creating a community for CBE innovators, where these leaders can collectively build capacity, remove barriers, and increase demand for high-quality CBE credentials. The American Institute for Research is conducting a survey of the higher education landscape to determine the current state of the field. An update on the adoption and scaling of CBE will be more evident when these survey results are released and posted online at www.cbenetwork.org in early 2018.

To help other institutions build their capacity for work in this area, C-BEN hosts its annual CBExchange, the only conference that's dedicated exclusively to the design, development, implementation, and scale-up of high-quality CBE programs. (See www.cbexchange.org for more information.) Held each fall, the conference has strong and diverse attendance, with well over 400 participants (C-BEN, 2016). At the 2016 event, half of all institutional attendees represented public institutions, with one quarter of attendees coming from private institutions, and another quarter coming from for-profit institutions. Over 40% of institutional attendees were from comprehensive colleges, with over a third coming from community colleges. Although one in five attendees were in the scale-up phase of CBE adoption, four in five attendees were seeking assistance in the planning, design, and implementation of new CBE programs.

The sustainability and growth of the movement depends on the collective action of leaders from all institutions and education stakeholders, as is evidenced by C-BEN. By working together, these leaders have already accomplished much. For example, the Technical Interoperability Pilot project, led by Mark Leuba, paired educators with vendors as they sought to find solutions to the significant technology challenges and barriers CBE programs face from adoption through scale-up (Leuba, 2015). Then, these institutions worked together to create the *Quality Framework for Competency-Based Education Programs*, released in September 2017 (C-BEN, 2017b). The framework establishes eight elements of quality that should be present in every competency-based program. Each element includes a principle statement that describes the fundamental proposition that provides the chain of reasoning behind the element. Then, a set of standards is provided so the element can be measured and comparatively evaluated. The framework then provides performance indicators that describe how effectively an institution is achieving the principle and standard. These performance indicators serve as a development guide to institutions seeking to build a new program or improve an existing one (C-BEN, 2017b). The *Quality Framework* strives to protect learners and the CBE movement from bad actors by serving as guideposts and guardrails for institutional leaders, policymakers, and accreditors. This book incorporates these principles and standards into the chapters that follow.

INSTITUTIONAL
CULTURE

Designing, building, launching, and continuously improving a high-quality competency-based education (CBE) program will affect the entire organization. Whether the institution is large or small, part of a larger system or freestanding, each phase of development will generate and present unique challenges to many departments within the institution, and a clear sense of institutional commitment will be essential to the success of the CBE program. This chapter will review some of the essential components of the sustained success of a CBE program, including a clear, steady, and deep commitment to the success of this initiative; integration of this effort into the overall university strategic plan; development of an institutional culture that supports responsible innovation; transparency regarding budget and operational planning; and a clear technology road map to support the work.

Deep Commitment

If an institution of higher education decides to consider design, development, and implementation of a CBE program, this effort must be rooted in a deep organizational commitment. This commitment has to be built on a realistic expectation about the big picture return on investment (ROI) for a CBE program to this particular institution. Desrochers and Staisloff (2016) offered a sobering overview regarding financial ROI for CBE programs, but this is just one component of an overall institutional analysis.

Institutions need to articulate a clear set of "returns" (in addition to financial returns) for the extensive investment required to offer a sustainable CBE program. Such additional ROIs might include enhanced institutional reputation, institutional morale boosting (due to the ability to innovate), or improved ability to serve learners.

Because a CBE program has the potential to challenge work processes and policies across the entire college or university, leaders at all levels have to understand the organization's degree of commitment for this work. More specifically, if the consistent message from the board, the president, and all senior leaders is that the CBE program represents an important priority, faculty and staff from across the organization will bring a solution mind-set to the development conversations. However, if the level of prioritization and commitment is unclear, the challenges to the status quo presented by a CBE program will appear insurmountable. This will result in interdepartmental struggles, and the new initiative will not gain traction. Even after an innovative program is launched, leadership vision and rationale for these innovative programs are essential to resist the "pull" to return to traditional higher education. In fact, there are several examples of institutions that initiated innovative competency-based programs in the 1970s but were defeated by the operational challenges of implementation at scale.

One case study can be found in an institution that was founded in a competency-based format as a university-without-walls within a larger state system. This institution evolved from a small base of passionate innovators into a growing organization that needed to hire new faculty and staff to keep up with student demand. As new faculty and staff were hired, however, the institution took for granted that these new community members would be committed to the same innovative vision, despite the fact that the 1990s were a very different era from the 1970s. Many of these new faculty and staff did not share (or perhaps understand) the original vision. As a new president and other institutional leaders joined, this original passion and commitment was not carried forward. Because of this shift, many of the policies and practices (that supported the competency-based model) began to erode. As leadership of the institution continues to change, bringing with it a more traditional institutional vision, the university marginalized the competency-based program into a small component of the overall university. Despite the deep experience in CBE, this university has not been able to benefit from the current interest because of an inconsistent and unclear institutional commitment to this innovation. This example demonstrates the power of vision in institutional commitment to change and the strength of the tendency to return to traditional programs in higher education.

Strategic Alignment

It is well documented that the landscape for institutions of higher education (IHEs) has changed significantly in the past decade. Jamie Merisotis (2015b), author of *America Needs Talent* (2015a) and president and CEO of the Lumina Foundation, stated the need as follows:

> The profile of today's college-going population looks much different than it did decades ago, when the average student was a fresh-faced 18-year-old moving directly from high school to campus. Students today are older, more experienced in work, and more socioeconomically and racially diverse than their peers of decades past. (para. 1)

It is precisely this shift that has challenged most colleges and universities to consider new strategies to achieve their vision and mission. CBE offers a value proposition to the new college-going population that has strong appeal: transparency of learning, flexibility, personalization, affordability, and employer-aligned competencies. If these benefits can be delivered effectively, CBE programs could have the potential to sustain the college or university into the future.

Within this context, however, the IHE must consider the impact of launching CBE programs on its overall strategic direction. Are the proposed CBE programs part of an organizational pivot to serve a new population of learners? Is this an effort to better serve the current set of learners? Will the proposed CBE program extend beyond current institutional disciplinary expertise? Does the launch of this program fundamentally shift the vision and mission for the college or university? Will the accreditors and other regulators understand how this new CBE program makes sense for this IHE?

The successful IHE will have a clearly articulated rationale for the movement into CBE programs. This rationale will articulate the linkage between the CBE program and the institution's vision/mission, suggesting either spots of synergy or areas of expansion, alongside clear reasons.

For institutions such as Brandman University or the University of Maryland University College, with a vision of serving adult students, CBE programming can directly align to the mission of the university. For other institutions, such as the University of Wisconsin–Milwaukee, the strategic alignment is more directly linked to their commitment to offer educational opportunities for professions needed in their region rather than the population of learners being served. In both examples, however, the CBE program's alignment to the institution's vision and mission can be easily explained and documented.

Institutional Culture

"Organizational culture eats strategy for breakfast, lunch, and dinner." This phrase is commonly attributed to Peter Drucker, and many other authors have written about the significance of this concept (Rizkalla, 2016). This phrase is intended to convey the importance of building an intentional structure to support responsible innovation (see Figure 1.1).

Creating a culture supportive of strategic innovation requires that institutional leaders who committed to a CBE program develop their own competencies as "change leaders" within the

Figure 1.1. Organizational culture eats strategy for breakfast, lunch, and dinner.

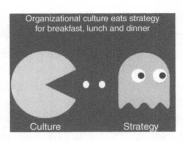

Note. From "Organizational Culture Eats Strategy for Breakfast, Lunch and Dinner," by T. Rick, 2014, *Meliorate,* www.torbenrick.eu/blog/culture/organisational-culture-eats-strategy-for-breakfast-lunch-and-dinner/

organization. In fact, everyone involved in creating the CBE program—from the board and institutional president to the IT help desk—ought to consider himself or herself to be a change leader. The culture has to shift to support collaboration and shared leadership toward the goal of providing an excellent CBE program to the targeted learners. In the words of Ward (2013), "We must find ways to stimulate and scale change across the institutions—as well as to sustain those changes—if we are to create models that can serve the expanding needs of our learners" (p. 22).

Change leadership, along with a clearly defined sense of the organizational ROI for the CBE program, forms a solid foundation for a new institutional culture based in responsible innovation. In a culture of responsible innovation, each team member considers how to achieve the larger organizational goal (e.g., launching a CBE program) with quality and within necessary limitations. This problem-solving mind-set (rather than a simple compliance mind-set) is the cornerstone of responsible innovation. In other words, rather than saying "We can't do that," an engaged change leader (at any level of the organization) operating in a culture of responsible innovation would say, "Let me think how we can get that done; here are some options with pros and cons to each." Within a culture of responsible innovation, faculty and staff are supported in taking reasonable and informed risks toward a well-defined goal (e.g., the launch of a CBE program).

Interestingly enough, one of the biggest sources of resistance might come from others who have created innovative programs in the institution. As Clayton Christenson (2011) described in *The Innovator's Dilemma*, people who have previously developed solutions to a challenge (e.g., improving delivery of higher education) can be the most resistant to additional changes, as they have come to believe strongly in the worth of their original solution. This problem can require a unique engagement strategy to gain support for the CBE program from these important thought leaders.

Budget and Planning Processes

A realistic and aligned budget, complete with financial targets, is essential to the ongoing success of a CBE effort. Because one of the promises of most CBE programs is to reduce the cost of higher education to students, it is essential that the decision of pricing (tuition, fees, and other student costs) is integrated with a testable financial model. In some cases, institutions have set a price point without a thoroughly delineated business model, and this has put pressure on these programs to scale more quickly than is practical. Because the shift away from time as a primary measure of student progess has a pervasive impact on institutional processes and practices, investments in new infrastructure and fundamental changes in work flows, policies, and business processes and systems are required. This means that the up-front costs of creating and offering a quality CBE program must be well understood in the budgeting and planning process.

Desrochers and Staisloff (2016) offered an insightful review of the emerging business models in four institutions offering CBE programs. It is clear from their work that institutions should not enter into the CBE arena hoping for a quick profit. In fact, it seems as though patience and clear performance targets are essential institutional characteristics when offering CBE programs. Desrochers and Staisloff (2016) found that the four CBE programs they reviewed expect to spend an average of $3,200 per student once their programs mature. However, program spending averaged $52,500 per student during the launch year. They also stated, "By the sixth year of operation, these four institutions anticipate that, on average, their CBE programs will be operating at half the cost of their traditional academic programs" (p. 6). Clearly, there is promise in these models, but there is significant investment required in the early years to support the shift away from time to competency demonstration.

It is also important to note that the behavior of students in these programs is still not well understood. It appears that students value these programs for the following primary reasons: (a) flexibility and (b) freedom to move quickly. In addition, many CBE programs are based on a subscription model of payment. The combination of the subscription model and the differing student pathways to a credential makes forecasting tuition revenue challenging. Retention and graduation rates will be different and will require a different formula to monitor.

In addition, if institutions adopt a new faculty model, offer student access on a subscription-based model, or move to a nonterm financial aid model, their faculty workload and pay model will be deeply affected. This will require ongoing analysis and adjustment to create a system that fits an institution's culture and satisfies the needs of students and regulators in this new model. Early engagement with the shared governance process at the institution will be essential to success when adapting or changing faculty workload and/or pay models.

Road Map: Technology and Product

Many creators of CBE programs envision a new model that is free from meeting seat time requirements, leverages student–faculty interaction just in time and regularly, delivers financial aid in incentivizing ways, transcribes competencies, and offers progression dashboards to both students and faculty. Each of these elements is challenging to deliver, in part because higher education's enabling technologies have been designed and built on different requirements and assumptions. Thus, institutions will do well to have a vision for their future CBE program toward which they can build incrementally. A fully vetted and agreed-on product road map can help prioritize the changes needed from the technology systems used by the university. The product road map will help all participants understand the bigger picture so that they can see how the work they are currently doing moves the academic program toward the future-state vision. It is also important because as compromises are made and priorities are set, the longer term, end-state vision can help keep the project on track—even as setbacks occur.

Technology vendors supply solutions when both the program requirements and the product demands are clear. Leuba (2015) summarized an early effort to support clarification of the requirements and incent vendors to develop prototype solutions. He described the five use cases that emerged from his survey of CBE institutions:

1. *Managing competencies using a unique key, in an integrated database, including the course-competency relationships.* The goal here is to be able to track students' demonstration of competency, controlling for version changes and moving beyond simple tracking of "courses" completed.

2. *Reporting assessment evaluation results between a learning management system or assessment platform and the student information system or system of record.* A solution to this use case would allow results from an assessment of competency to be captured in the learning management system (or other assessment platform) and transferred to the student information system—or whatever system the institution currently uses to capture grades. Because grades are different from the methods programs use to label competency demonstration, this is a critical component for the scalability of CBE programs.

3. *Extracting CBE program information for nonterm–based financial aid.* Federal financial aid offers the nonterm financial aid option, and this option comes with a number of requirements. For example, the institution must track the number of competencies successfully demonstrated as a proportion of the overall required competencies for the credential being earned. This is different from tracking the number of credits earned by passing courses, and it requires new solutions.

4. *Measuring components of regular and substantive interaction.* Another important requirement for federal financial aid in CBE programs is the need for regular and substantive interaction between the faculty and the students in the program. Institutions will be required to monitor this and to take action when it is not occurring. Although this is possible to do manually, a technology-enabled solution is essential to the scaling of these programs.

5. *Producing an extended CBE e-transcript.* One of the value propositions central to CBE programming is the transparency of demonstrated competencies—to the learner and other constituents. Traditional transcripts list courses, credits, and grades. CBE-based transcripts need to list the competencies earned, but they also need to offer a "crosswalk" back to credit hours and grades to enable learners' goals such as transfer, employer reimbursement, and additional education. Most current transcripts do not easily offer these capabilities (Leuba, 2015).

Following the development of these use cases, Leuba (2015) successfully engaged with a group of educational technology providers to develop prototype solutions for each of these challenges. The prototypes were reviewed by participating institutions, and this feedback was incorporated into the emerging technology solutions.

The following are the important takeaways from Leuba's (2015) work: (a) the realization that there are some shared technology needs across the diversity of CBE programs and (b) the fact that once these use cases were created, vendors participated in mocking up potential solutions. This suggests that when the CBE field is able to define its needs clearly, the market will provide workable solutions. For the institutional leader, this suggests the need to collaborate with other institutions (through organizations such as the Competency-Based Education Network or other means) to support the ability of important vendors to generate solutions. This is another reason for institutions to work to specify where technology hurdles and roadblocks exist and to be able to share this information across institutions and encourage solution development by vendors.

Conclusion

In summary, there are very few corners of the university that will remain untouched by the decision to launch a CBE program. Unique challenges will arise from each of these constituents, and unique engagement strategies must be designed to support all constituents in adoption of the vision for the CBE program. A clear, steady, and deep commitment to the CBE program is central to its ultimate success. In addition, it will be important to offer clarity for the university community regarding how the CBE program fits into the overall university strategic plan. Leaders must intentionally work to develop an institutional culture that supports responsible innovation while providing transparency regarding budget and operational planning and articulating a clear technology road map to support the work.

2

PROGRAM DESIGN

What should leaders know about competency-based education (CBE) program design? What are the initial big picture decisions that need to be determined? How can CBE programs be built to ensure student success? These critical components of program design and pivotal decisions will provide a foundation for building a program that ensures learners' success. In this chapter, we will explore the following program design topics:

- Delivery model
- Program selection
- Backward design
- Deconstruction-reconstruction and framework origin
- Orientation and program fit

Delivery Model

One of the first steps in designing a CBE program is to consider the delivery model of the program. CBE programs may be offered in one modality or in a combination of modalities that include fully online, blended (combination of online and on-ground), and fully on-ground.

Determining the best modality for a CBE program depends on several factors such as institutional culture, experience in use of technology for teaching and learning, institutional mission and vision, program of study, and market and demand needs (i.e., local, national, and/or international reach of the program). Modality must be considered at the beginning of the program design, as it affects how faculty and staff engage and support students, curriculum development, pedagogical teaching and learning approaches, and needed resources (i.e., online learning platform and instructional designers).

Delivery Model Queries

Here are some general questions and areas of inquiry for you to consider as a starting point in choosing a delivery model. It might be helpful to engage in group discussion with your institutional team, or you could assign this as a pregroup meeting reflective exercise. You could ask participants to review the questions and write responses, thoughts, and additional questions ahead of the meeting in hopes to have full engagement and be able to broaden the discussion.

1. What is your institutional mission and vision? How does this relate to or guide teaching and learning at your institution?
2. How would you describe your institutional culture, especially in regard to change?
3. When you think about a recent change or innovative initiative at your institution, do you know if there are lessons learned, pitfalls, and successes?
4. What is the level of use and comfort with technology for teaching for faculty and learners?
5. What program and/or discipline are you considering for CBE?
6. Does this proposed program require some face-to-face instruction such as internships, clinical experience, apprenticeships, lab work, and so on?
7. Does this proposed program require approval by a professional accreditor? If so, are there requirements or guidelines to consider for the delivery model?
8. What are the market and demand needs of the program (i.e., local, national, and/or international)?

To ensure a robust discussion, we suggest that this group reflection include a cross section of positions and disciplines. It would be helpful to capture this "group think" in a summary document, as this may be referenced throughout your journey of building a CBE program. Likely down the road, the university will need to justify its delivery model choice to a broader audience of faculty, administrators, and staff, as well as accreditors, state departments, and possibly at the federal level.

After this group discussion, you may have many more questions, and that is an excellent sign that you are thinking deeply and widely. Keep a running log of questions, as it will be essential as you design an engaging and supportive competency-based program. This is also a great beginning step in developing a "frequently asked questions" (FAQ) document, which may come in handy for later presentations on your CBE program.

Delivery Model Characteristics

Although there are many considerations, there are two main characteristics to think about in CBE delivery models. The first characteristic is the range of the student experience from a fully online program to a fully in-person program. For example, in a fully online program, the student engages with the curriculum, with peers, with faculty, and with advisers (coaches) in an online environment. Fully online programs use technology for delivering the program, and faculty and coaches connect and support students in a virtual setting (i.e., online modules and meetings), whereas a fully in-person program may require students to attend regularly scheduled learning labs to work on competencies. In addition, a fully in-person program may also require a real-life experiential component such as clinical, internship, practicum, student teaching, and so on.

The second delivery characteristic to consider is the range of time from high to low flexibility. A program with low flexibility in time may require that learners complete a set amount of competencies within a given period of time such as a semester or session. This type of program has a beginning and an end date, though students may set their own pace within this specific time frame. A program with high flexibility in time allows students to set their own pace of learning without a true "end." In this high-flexibility program, students can take a month or a year to complete a competency. Following are some case study examples of an institution's delivery model.

Case Study Examples

Fully online and high flexibility. University One currently offers a CBE undergraduate degree program that is fully online. Learners are enrolled in online competency modules (i.e., courses) and can start their program on any Monday. Learners complete the competency-based program at their own pace and move from one bundle of competencies to another upon successful mastery of the content. Students are not required to complete their competencies at the end of a predetermined time frame such as semester.

Partially online and medium flexibility. University Two offers a CBE associate's degree program that has all of the courses online and requires an internship experience. While learners are completing their online competency work, they are engaged in person in a supervised job-related internship where they practice and demonstrate their knowledge, skills, and abilities. Learners must complete their assigned competencies and internship experience within semester time frames.

Fully in-person and medium flexibility. University Three offers a CBE undergraduate certificate program that requires students to attend the learning lab a minimum of 20 hours per week. Students can choose 18 out of 20 hours that are best for their schedule. (The lab is open 45 hours a week Monday through Saturday with evening hours and morning hours.) Students must attend a predetermined 2-hour block each week to ensure all students meet synchronously with the faculty member. Students can work at their own pace in completing the competencies but must complete the whole amount of competencies assigned by the end of the semester.

Delivery Model Recommendation

As you are discovering, there is a lot to consider in determining the best delivery model. After working with your institutional team, you can start to outline the proposed delivery model in regard to (a) student experience (i.e., fully online, in-person, combination, internships, labs, etc.) and (b) high to low flexibility in regard to time (i.e., time limits to complete competencies). It is suggested that you document and describe the institution's recommended delivery model with justifications and a listing of team participants (names, titles, offices). This document will help with future planning, vetting, and approval processes both internally and externally (i.e., regional accreditor, state department of education, etc.).

Program Selection

Selecting a CBE program is based on many factors, whether it is the institution's first CBE program or an additional program. For starters, institutions will need to determine the level of the program (i.e., certificate, baccalaureate, master's, or doctoral) and the discipline (i.e., business, information technology, liberal arts, or nursing). If an institution decides to build a baccalaureate degree, it will need to decide the student entry level (admissions) for the CBE program. For example, some universities' CBE programs include general education in addition to the major, whereas some institutions build the last two years of a baccalaureate degree and require students to complete their associate's degree prior to admission.

Let's walk through some considerations and suggestions to help you decide the best CBE program for your institution.

Market and Demand Research

Institutions commonly conduct market and demand research to determine the best CBE program to offer. This may include a national-level analysis if the program is to be offered online nationwide, or the research may be limited to a local job market. Through research of industry and labor analytics, institutions are assessing for the viability of a program by conducting a thorough review.

A competitive analysis is commonly conducted to see what CBE programs other institutions are offering. Because there are a limited number of CBE programs, this analysis could include institutions that offer credit-hour programs that are trending up in the job market. Information gathered in the competitive analysis may include the following:

- Name of the institution and contact information
- Program title

- Number of credits in the program (or competencies if it is a CBE program)
- Delivery model
- Admission criteria
- Description of degree requirements
- Number of students in the program
- Number of graduates
- Any unique factors in the program (i.e., internship, employer, mentor, etc.)

In addition, research and demand analysis may also be conducted to determine job markets. This analysis may include a review of national job posting data for a targeted program for short- and long-term projections. Though there are several approaches to obtain these data, Burning Glass Technologies provides a robust labor analytics tool. In addition, relevant O*NET (U.S. Department of Labor, Employment, and Training Administration's Occupational Information Network) occupational codes can be used to conduct a review of job postings and opportunities for graduates of a targeted program. Occupational projections and trends are analyzed to determine viability and sustainability of the program over time.

Market and demand analysis will help the institution answer the following questions:

1. What programs and/or credentials are supported by market research?
2. Is there a workforce need for the CBE program?
3. What competency-based programs are competitors currently offering?
4. Is the program viable?
5. Is the program sustainable? If yes, for how long?
6. Are there special considerations in determining the development and offering of a CBE program (i.e., delivery model, length of program, admissions requirements, unique characteristics, etc.)?

Institution's Mission, Vision, and Strategic Direction

Alignment of the proposed CBE program with the institution's mission, vision, and strategic plan is a critical piece in program selection. How does the proposed CBE program fit in the institution? For example, institutions whose mission and vision encompass areas such as innovating, meeting the needs of underserved students, and preparing graduates for the workforce may find that CBE is well aligned to their mission, vision, and strategic direction. Or an institution may decide to expand in new areas such as health care and feel that CBE is a viable delivery model to open new avenues.

School, College, Department, and Faculty

Dependent on the institution, the factors of program offerings and the culture of specific schools, colleges, or departments may influence the program selection. In addition, some faculty members may be excited about the opportunity to build and offer a CBE program, whereas others may not. For example, when one university was determining which program of study should be its first CBE program, faculty from two schools (i.e., education and business) were vying for the opportunity to be the one to offer the institution's first CBE program. Each school proposed its program to the provost, who made the final decision based on its interest (and the demand analysis). (In case you are wondering, the school of education was chosen at this institution.)

Some institutions have a go-to school, college, or department that is eager for innovating and creating new ways for teaching and learning. In this case, it might be easier to build a CBE program if one knows that the faculty are onboard from the beginning. This particular unit may also have the background and experience (i.e., discipline outcome frameworks and assessment) for building a new CBE program that would be immensely helpful.

A fascinating and effective approach for selecting a college was initiated at Purdue University. President Mitch Daniels posed a university-wide challenge for the first college to build a CBE program. The award of $500,000 was granted to the College of Technology for a proposal to create a transdisciplinary bachelor's degree.

Strategies vary widely across institutions in determining the fit of building a CBE program in a particular school, college, or department. The engagement and commitment of the faculty, administrators, and staff will help to ensure successful creation and implementation of a CBE program. This cannot be a "force-fed" initiative but should be one of invitation with an eager and creative team.

Backward Design

The Understanding by Design framework is a planning process and structure that guides curriculum, assessment, and instruction that "1) focus on teaching and assessing for understanding and learning transfer, and 2) design curriculum 'backward' from those ends" (McTighe & Wiggins, 2012, p. 1). The curriculum is planned backward from the desired results to evidence of learning to the learning plan.

These desired results, also known as *competency statements*, represent *deep learning* that involves big ideas that give meaning and importance to knowledge and facts. It is the deep learning that allows learners to transfer knowledge from one topic to another, from one competency to another, from module learning to life.

This "beginning with the end in mind" backward design approach differs from a more traditional approach in that assessments are created prior to developing the curriculum (i.e., the learning journey). In a traditional approach, the learning journey (which includes learning activities such as reading assignments, projects, practice activities, etc.) is normally developed prior to the assessments.

An example of the traditional approach is how a course such as statistics is taught. After outlining the learning materials, exercises, activities, and problems, an instructor would then write an exam to test students' knowledge. The creation of the assessment followed the creation of the learning journey. We are accustomed (at least I was) to developing these learning activities, assigning reading materials, and preparing presentations and lecture materials *before* creating the assessment of student knowledge. By creating the assessments *prior* to the educational journey, one can ensure that the learning activities and materials are clearly aligned to the competency and supporting learning objectives (see Table 2.1).

TABLE 2.1
Comparison of Traditional and Backward Design Steps

Step	Traditional Approach	Backward Design
1	Write competency statements and objectives	Write competency statements and objectives
2	Develop learning journey and activities	Create assessments
3	Create assessments	Develop learning journey and activities

Creating a CBE program opens the door for a new approach to teaching and learning. A CBE leader might find it helpful to engage in discussion with faculty about backward design, teaching, and learning. Backward design was initially used in a K–12 environment and is less known in postsecondary fields. Although some faculty may be knowledgeable about backward design, it would be beneficial to discuss and explore its merits and benefits for CBE program design.

Though backward design is widely practiced and an accepted approach in building a CBE program across institutions, there is a difference in how institutions develop the structure of the CBE program through its areas of study and competency statements. How does an institution build a CBE program? In the next section, we will explore two common approaches for creating a CBE program: deconstruction-reconstruction and framework origin.

Deconstruction-Reconstruction and Framework Origin

When an institution is building a CBE program for a certificate, associate's, baccalaureate, master's, or doctoral program, its approach in building the foundation of the program (i.e., competency statements) is to take an existing credit-hour program and break it apart and rebuild it (deconstruction-reconstruction) or create a program based on frameworks, standards, and/or principles (framework origin). Awareness of these approaches will assist CBE leaders in guiding faculty and other curriculum creators to where to start (deconstruction-reconstruction and framework origin). In addition, a step-by-step guide will be provided to help leaders guide the team in building the foundation for their CBE program.

Deconstruction-Reconstruction

The deconstruction-reconstruction approach is a common way for institutions to build a CBE program. This approach uses current curricula, degree requirements, course descriptions, and supporting learning objectives as the starting point.

Faculty deconstruct, or take apart (not implode like they do buildings in Vegas), an existing degree piece by piece (learning outcome by learning outcome) for each required course. These "bite-size" outcomes are normally those listed in a syllabus (i.e., course objective or course outcomes), which are then reorganized into new categories or "buckets." With this approach, you have the same puzzle pieces, but you are creating a new picture with them. These new categories or groupings of outcomes change the structure of the degree from the preexisting required courses to new groupings of outcomes that equate to a competency. See Table 2.2 for basic steps to building a CBE program using the deconstruction-reconstruction approach.

The deconstruction-reconstruction approach is much like taking a building apart piece by piece and making a new structure using most of the same pieces, though one can get rid of redundant pieces, improve a piece (rewrite an outcome), and add new pieces based on stakeholder input or discovery of a missing piece of learning. This new structure may be more streamlined, integrated, efficient, and effective with the new groupings of learning and the sequencing of the competencies.

Framework Origin

Another approach for building a CBE program is to use existing standards, principles, or frameworks, known as the *framework origin approach*. The program selected will guide the CBE team in selecting the appropriate frameworks.

For example, some disciplines have specific standards and outcomes, such as professional organizations in the areas of nursing, engineering, teaching, psychology, and social work. Other frameworks exist in career and technical fields with specified areas of study and outcomes, as well as industry standard certifications. There are also frameworks in liberal arts and twenty-first-century skills. Fortunately, there is also a rich source of information on

TABLE 2.2

Deconstruction-Reconstruction Approach to CBE

Step	Description	Notes and Suggestions
1	Write each course learning outcome on a separate strip of paper. Do this for each course required in a degree program.	Consider putting each course learning outcome on sticky paper, which will permit moving it from category to category for subsequent steps. You may wish to make these a bigger font or handwritten large to ensure one can see them from 5 to 6 feet away.
2	Code each course learning outcome to track its original source (e.g., course discipline, course number, and outcome number).	It is important to establish a coding system (e.g., course system, course number, and outcome number) so you can look for gaps or check for clarity at a later date. Keep a spreadsheet of these outcomes, and write codes on the back of each course outcome strip. An example for a Psychology 101 course with five outcomes could be P101-1 for the first outcome, P101-2 for the second outcome, and so on.
3	Each outcome now "lives" on its own. Check spreadsheet coding and individual course outcomes and codes for accuracy.	This is detailed work, and it is easy to miss a piece of learning or miscode an outcome. Take the time to do a quality check. It will save you many hours later on.
4	Group related outcomes into groups or categories. Think about what pieces of learning or bundles of learning go together.	Butcher-size paper on the wall of a large room will greatly facilitate this exercise. It is helpful to have the outcomes randomly given to a group of faculty to start this process. It is so easy to go back to the "course" and end up with the same construction as the original. And no cheating! No catalogs or course syllabi in the room (just a suggestion).

(Continues)

TABLE 2.2 *(Continued)*

Step	Description	Notes and Suggestions
5	Write an overarching competency statement that addresses all of the individual outcomes. Note that sometimes one of the outcomes in the group may serve as the overarching outcome.	This is hard work, and it is important to have a small group of faculty working together in writing the competency statements. It is helpful to have resources such as Bloom's taxonomy available for faculty. Through this exercise some of the outcomes may be moved to other categories or discarded if they are redundant. This will likely take a few iterations, with some gaps in time to reflect on the work.
6	Ensure alignment of the individual outcomes in this category by making revisions to statements for clarity, measurability, and appropriate level of learning.	Once the overarching competency statements are written, faculty can take a closer look at the outcome statements. Remember that these came from the syllabi, and this is a great opportunity to improve the outcomes for clarity and alignment to the competency statement. There may need to be additional outcomes written here to support the competency statement.
7	Share the competency statement and supporting outcomes with a stakeholder group for feedback. Make improvements and adjustments based on the feedback.	Dependent on the program, choose the most appropriate stakeholder groups to review the competency statement and the supporting outcomes. This could be employers, professionals in the field, and university internal stakeholder groups (i.e., advising, career services, teaching and learning centers).

(Continues)

TABLE 2.2 (*Continued*)

Step	Description	Notes and Suggestions
8	Bundle, sequence, and scaffold the competencies to create the program schedule.	This exercise is to create the schedule of the competencies. What should students take first? Are there competencies that are foundational (i.e., writing) that a student should have in the beginning of the program? Do you wish to have some flexibility in the order of the competencies or more of a set sequence? Think of this as how faculty currently set the schedule of course of study for students for degree completion.

required knowledge, skills, and abilities for specified professions in the U.S. Department of Labor's O*NET data.

In this section, we will illustrate the framework origin approach through exploration of frameworks, a university case study illustration, and steps for building a CBE program.

Selected frameworks. One of the frameworks used for undergraduate education is the Association of American Colleges & Universities (AAC&U) Liberal Education and America's Promise (LEAP) Essential Learning Outcomes. The outcome statements were written to meet the demands for more "college-educated workers and more engaged and informed citizens" (AAC&U, 2018). The Essential Learning Outcomes fall in the following overarching areas:

1. Knowledge of human cultures and the physical and natural world
2. Intellectual and practical skills
3. Personal and social responsibility
4. Integrative and applied learning

The AAC&U continued this good work by creating rubrics for assessing outcomes in each of these areas. See Figure 2.1 for a more in-depth view of the AAC&U Essential Learning Outcomes.

Figure 2.1. AAC&U Essential Learning Outcomes.

Knowledge of human cultures and the physical and natural world

- Through study in the sciences and mathematics, social sciences, humanities, histories, languages, and the arts

Focused by engagement with big questions, both contemporary and enduring

Intellectual and practical skills, including

- Inquiry and analysis
- Critical and creative thinking
- Written and oral communication
- Quantitative literacy
- Information literacy
- Teamwork and problem solving

Practiced extensively, across the curriculum, in the context of progressively more challenging problems, projects, and standards for performance

Personal and social responsibility, including

- Civic knowledge and engagement—local and global
- Intercultural knowledge and competence
- Ethical reasoning and action
- Foundations and skills for lifelong learning

Anchored through active involvement with diverse communities and real-world challenges

Integrative and applied learning, including

- Synthesis and advanced accomplishment across general and specialized studies

Demonstrated through the application of knowledge, skills, and responsibilities to new settings and complex problems

---

Another framework for consideration is the Degree Qualifications Profile (Adelman, Ewell, Gaston, & Schneider, 2014, p. 45), commissioned by the Lumina Foundation, which outlines what all college students should know and be able to do at the associate's, bachelor's, and master's levels to prepare for twenty-first-century workforce needs in the following areas:

1. *Specialized knowledge.* This category focuses on the students' ability to demonstrate beyond vocabularies, theories, and skills in their chosen specialized area of study.
2. *Broad and integrative knowledge.* This category is about what students can discover, explore (e.g., concepts), and question that bridges and consolidates essential areas of learning across different broad fields of study (e.g., humanities, arts, sciences).
3. *Intellectual skills.* This category emphasizes analytical inquiry, use of information resources, engagement with different perspectives, ethical reasoning, quantitative fluency, and communicative fluency.
4. *Applied and collaborative learning.* This category focuses on what students can do with what they know through addressing unscripted problems at work and settings outside of the classroom.
5. *Civic and global learning.* This category emphasizes students' integration of knowledge and skills by engaging with and responding to civic, social, environmental, and economic challenges at local, national, and global levels.

The Degree Qualifications Profile is used frequently as a framework in undergraduate CBE programs. Many institutions in the Competency-Based Education Network (C-BEN) have used the Degree Qualifications Profile as a framework for their CBE programs.

The framework of industry standards is also used for targeted CBE programs. This is especially helpful, if not required, for many programs that are tightly aligned to existing professional standards. Industry standards can come in the form of specific outcomes outlined in a program of study and standardized certification examinations such as IT certifications in A+, Network+, and CompTIA Cloud Essentials.

Databases of knowledge, skills, and abilities for specified careers and professions are a deep robust pool of outcomes for framing competencies for a CBE program. A superb example is the

U.S. Department of Labor's O*NET database, which lists hundreds of occupational definitions and learning outcomes associated with specific jobs. In addition, many professions (e.g., nurses, counselors, teachers, and engineers) outline specific standards and outcomes for which students must demonstrate competency.

Brandman University case study. Brandman University built a competency-based Bachelor of Science in Information Technology (BSIT) that encompasses the major areas of computer information systems and technologies, programming and software development, networks, operating systems, databases, security, cloud computing, web design, project management, and business intelligence and data analytics. In addition to the IT content, the competency-based BSIT program includes general education requirements and mobile skills demanded by employers across all professions of leadership, team building, conflict management, organizational dynamics, and ethics and social responsibility.

The Brandman University general education competencies are based on the AAC&U's LEAP Essential Learning Outcomes and the Lumina Foundation's Degree Qualifications Profile (DQP) as a basis for establishing liberal arts and twenty-first-century competencies. As a result, the competency framework included outcomes in the areas of (a) applied learning, (b) innovation and creativity, (c) civic engagement, (d) global cultures, and (e) integrated learning.

The program also used industry-endorsed certifications from CompTIA, CIW, and Microsoft and the U.S. Department of Labor's O*NET database as frameworks to build the competency framework. Figure 2.2 illustrates the various frameworks for Brandman University's competency-based BSIT program.

Framework origin approach step-by-step process. The steps for the framework origin may appear to be simple in description, but they are truly rich and deep work, starting with the end in mind. On the basis of one or more frameworks, standards, databases, industry standard certifications, and so on, the faculty are answering the question "What should students know, understand, and be able to do at the end of the program?" If the faculty are using more than one framework, they are called to integrate the various structures into a meaningful, cohesive, competency-based structure. See Table 2.3 for steps to building a CBE program using the framework origin approach.

Figure 2.2. Framework origin for Brandman University's CBE Bachelor of Science in Information Technology (BSIT) program.

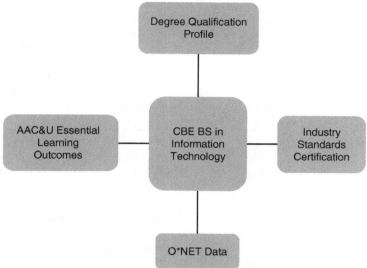

Note. AAC&U = Association of American Colleges & Universities.

Summary

The deconstruction-reconstruction approach builds on existing, predefined structures or outcomes in a program to rebuild it into a CBE program, whereas the framework origin approach uses various frameworks to build the CBE program, permitting a fresh perspective of the degree program. It should be noted that some institutions may decide to use a combination approach using existing program outcomes (deconstruction-reconstruction) and adding or overlaying a framework. It is important that the CBE leaders review these approaches with their institutional team to determine the best approach. This is an exciting step in creating the foundation for a CBE program.

Orientation and Program Fit

There is one more area that an institution may wish to consider about program design. Does the institution wish to create

TABLE 2.3
Framework Origin Approach to Competency-Based Education

Step	Description	Notes and Suggestions
1	Review relevant frameworks, standards, principles, databases, and industry standard certifications and choose an appropriate framework or frameworks.	This will take some time and research by faculty and other subject matter experts such as professionals in the field and/or employers. The institution may also wish to include current and future trends in the field. Is the field rapidly changing? If so, how can this be incorporated in the program?
2	List each of the outcomes, standards and knowledge, skills, and abilities on a separate strip of paper.	Some of the outcomes or standards may be "packed" with multiple outcomes. At this time it may be helpful to break these into smaller components.
3	Code each outcome to track its original source (e.g., framework, standards, principles, database, etc.).	Establishing a coding system with the original source is important to ensure you can go back and check for clarity and look for gaps. Keep a spreadsheet of these outcomes, and write codes on the back of each outcome strip. An example is DQP AL1 for Degree Qualifications Profile Applied Learning Outcome #1.
4	Group related outcomes into groups or categories. Think about what pieces of learning or bundles of learning go together.	Butcher-size paper on the wall of a large room will greatly facilitate this exercise. It is helpful to have the outcomes randomly given to a group of faculty to start this process.
5	Write an overarching competency statement that addresses all of the individual outcomes. Note that sometimes one of the outcomes in the group may serve as the overarching outcome.	This is hard work, and it is important to have a small group of faculty working together in writing the competency statements. It is helpful to have resources such as Bloom's taxonomy available for faculty. Through this exercise some of the outcomes may be moved to other categories or discarded if they are redundant. This will likely take a few iterations, with some gaps in time to reflect on the work.

(Continues)

TABLE 2.3 (*Continued*)

Step	Description	Notes and Suggestions
6	Ensure alignment of the individual outcomes in this category by making revisions to statements for clarity, measurability, and appropriate level of learning.	Once the overarching competency statements are written, faculty can take a closer look at the outcome statements. There may need to be additional outcomes written here to support the competency statement.
7	Share the competency statement and supporting outcomes with a stakeholder group for feedback. Make improvements and adjustments based on the feedback.	Dependent on the program, choose the most appropriate stakeholder groups to review the competency statement and the supporting outcomes. This could be employers, professionals in the field, and university internal stakeholder groups (i.e., advising, career services, teaching and learning centers).
8	Bundle, sequence, and scaffold the competencies to create the program schedule.	This exercise is to create the schedule of the competencies. What should students take first? Are there competencies that are foundational (i.e., writing) that a student should have in the beginning of the program? Do you wish to have some flexibility in the order of the competencies or more of a set sequence? Think of this as how faculty currently set the schedule of course of study for degree completion.

a student orientation or some program strategy to help prepare students for a CBE program and assess for "fit"?

CBE programs are relatively new and likely differ significantly from students' previous educational experience. Universities and colleges need to make sure students have clear information about expectations and requirements of the program and what the student experience looks like. Students need to answer the question, "Is this the right program for me?"

Universities and colleges must actively describe what students will be expected to do in a CBE program. According to Baker

(2015), "Online videos, quizzes, student testimonials, and materials from the programs allow students to explore programs before enrolling" (p. 4). These approaches can also serve as a marketing tool for prospective students, though they may not always accurately reflect a true student experience in a CBE program. There are many approaches to help students determine if CBE is right for them.

For example, Western Governors University offers a 10-question quiz that asks questions such as the following: What kind of experience do you have that would apply to your course of study? Technology-based learning is pretty different from the classrooms of our childhood. How comfortable are you with that? and Do you have the support system in place at home and/or work to go back to school?

Another approach for aligning student fit with CBE is through a frequently asked question (FAQ) list. For instance, Northern Essex Community College (2017) has CBE FAQs posted on its website. FAQ question "Is CBE right for me?" states, "CBE courses are for busy students who can learn independently online. If you are self-motivated, eager to get your degree/certificate, and have work experience that you can apply to your learning, then CBE may be right for you."

Characteristics of learners are also used to determine fit of CBE programs, as found in *My College Guide* (2016), which cites the following:

> While these programs are designed to be an even more flexible option than online degrees, those who are the most successful in competency-based programs typically have the following characteristics:
>
> - Highly-motivated and self-driven
> - Extensive professional experience within their field
> - Independent learners
> - Ability to work at a fast-pace (para.14)

Through a variety of approaches and communication channels, universities and colleges are publishing and sharing clear expectations of the CBE program from the very beginning—when learners are first interested in the program. The nascent nature of CBE programs today necessitates clear messaging to learners to help determine fit for the program and gain an understanding of program requirements. In addition, institutional policies, tuition, fees, and processes must be clearly communicated to learners throughout their program.

Conclusion

For a CBE leader, the deep work with program design is enormously satisfying work. It is your opportunity to work with faculty and the full CBE team in building the architecture of the CBE program. Through discussion, reflection, and information, your institution addresses the delivery model, program selection, backward design, deconstruction-reconstruction and framework origin approachs, and orientation. There is additional information provided in chapter 7, "Approval Considerations," that will need to be addressed as part of the program design.

3

ASSESSMENT ESSENTIALS AND STRATEGIES

A distinctive feature of competency-based education (CBE) programs is the focus on the assessment of student learning. CBE programs are built with the foundational structure of sound, relevant, and rigorous assessments. Students must "pass" all summative assessments, each of which is built to demonstrate mastery. Leaders of CBE must have a deep understanding of assessment in CBE programs to help guide building a program and ensuring its quality. In this chapter, we will explore the following assessment essentials and strategies:

- Higher education assessment
- Assessment design principles
- Types and properties
- Program assessment project plan
- Building performance-based summative assessments and assignments
- Building objective-based assessments
- Quality assurance

Higher Education Assessment

Assessments provide evidence of what students know, are able to do, and can apply to authentic settings and situations. Assessment leader and author Linda Suskie (2015) stated that student learning assessment is really about answering the following questions:

- Do you have evidence that your students are achieving your key learning outcomes?
- Does the evidence meet the characteristics of good evidence?
- Are you using evidence to not only evaluate individual students but also improve what you are doing? (p. 151)

Higher education has developed and nurtured a culture of assessment over the past 20-plus years, as evidenced by the work and research of the National Institute for Learning Outcomes Assessment (NILOA); the Association of American Colleges Universities (AAC&U); and the tremendous growth in the number of assessment conferences, books, papers, and resources. Assessing student learning is required practice at accredited small, large, public, and private institutions. In addition, programs that hold professional accreditation status in fields such as nursing, engineering, business, and education require evidence of student learning and use of outcome data for program improvement.

In higher education, where the vast majority of programs are credit based (i.e., courses are typically 3 credits, a baccalaureate degree equates to 120 credits, etc.), universities are well versed in the assessment of student learning. At the course level, student learning as evidenced through projects, papers, and examinations is individually assessed to determine each student's level of achievement, usually resulting in a letter grade ranging from A (excellent) to F (failure). Other contributions to a student's overall grade may include student participation, discussion, attendance, and smaller assignments or quizzes. In a credit-hour program, students can pass an undergraduate course with an A, B, or C (and sometimes D). In the credit-hour model, each student's learning may vary, with the understanding that a student receiving an A learned more than a student who received a C grade.

In the competency-based world, one must be able to provide evidence that *each* student has mastered *each* competency. In a CBE program, learning is constant, which means that each student must master the competency by meeting or exceeding the minimum requirement for mastery (i.e., 80% or higher on an exam or proficiency at all criteria on a rubric) on the final assessment.

Students in competency-based assessment programs cannot fail one part (i.e., objective and/or criteria) of a competency and then do beautifully on another part and, therefore, "average" a mastery. Students in competency-based programs must demonstrate mastery on all parts of a competency. In addition, students must master all competencies in the program.

CBE leaders will be asked to guide the assessment planning and implementation for competency-based programs. To this end, it is helpful to understand how assessment strategies differ for competency-based programs. Throughout this chapter, we will explore assessment properties, types, and design, with practical guides and worksheets to facilitate the work.

Assessment Design Principles

The seminal piece for assessment principles and design was written over 25 years ago when the American Association for Higher Education's Assessment Forum released "Principles of Good Practice for Assessing Student Learning" (Astin, Banta, Cross, El-Khawas, Ewell, Hutchings et al., 1992), written by 12 academic practitioners. These principles have stood the test of time and continue to be cited on institutions' assessment websites as the guiding lights to assist in developing student learning outcomes. The nine overarching principles are as follows:

1. The assessment of student learning begins with educational values.
2. Assessment is most effective when it reflects an understanding of learning as multidimensional, integrated, and revealed in performance over time.
3. Assessment works best when the programs it seeks to have clear, explicitly stated purposes.
4. Assessment requires attention to outcomes but also and equally to the experiences that lead to those outcomes.
5. Assessment works best when it is ongoing, not episodic.
6. Assessment fosters wider improvement when representatives from across the educational community are involved.
7. Assessment makes a difference when it begins with issues of use and illuminates questions that people really care about.

8. Assessment is most likely to lead to improvement when it is part of a larger set of conditions that promote change.
9. Through assessment, educators meet responsibilities to students and to the public. (para. 6–14)

Through the eyes of a CBE leader, these principles can be used as a foundation for CBE assessment. Although many of these principles are relevant to CBE assessment with some adaptation, there are a few principles that stand prominently.

Principle 3 speaks to clarity, transparency, and purpose of a competency-based program. What will students know, understand, and be able to do? This calls for clear competency statements with aligned supportive objectives and coherent relevant assignments.

Principle 4 addresses the practice of developing competency-based programs through backward design, with competencies and assessment creation occurring before the curriculum and educational journey. In this way, curriculum and student activities are aligned to specific outcomes.

Principle 5 focuses on the need for formative assessment as part of a student's educational journey. It is this learning along the way that prepares a student for the summative assessment success.

Principle 6 originally called out inclusion of faculty, student affairs, librarians, administrators, and students to collaborate in creation and use of assessment. For the CBE world, this community would also include employers, human resource specialists, and professional accreditors.

Astin and colleague's nine "Principles of Good Practice for Assessing Student Learning" are not meant to be prescriptive, but they allow institutions a foundation on which to build their own assessment design principles for CBE, as noted in principles 4 through 6.

Another example of assessment principles is the Queen's University (2011) assessment policy, which lists 10 principles. This assessment policy broadens the assessment principles by including grading practices, transparency, and fairness. The Queen's University assessment policies are as follows:

1. Assessment practice should promote effective learning.
2. The amount and timing of assessment enables effective and appropriate evaluation of students' achievement of intended learning outcomes.

3. Appropriate and timely feedback is provided to students on assessed work in a way that promotes learning and facilitates improvement.
4. Students should be fully aware of what constitutes academic misconduct and the consequences associated with it.
5. Everyone involved in assessment of students must be competent to undertake their roles and responsibilities.
6. The principles and procedures for, and processes of, assessment should be explicit, valid, and reliable.
7. Assessment should be conducted with rigour, probity, and fairness and with due regard to security.
8. The procedures for marking and for moderating marks must be transparent and fair.
9. The criteria for progressing from one stage of a program to another and for qualifying for an award must be transparent.
10. Assessment decisions must be documented accurately and systematically, and decisions of relevant assessment panels and examination boards are to be communicated as quickly as possible.

The Queen's University assessment policies clearly highlight the obligation of assessment to be transparent in its intended learning outcomes, to be directly related to the objectives, and to be clear and understandable to students. Institutions must ensure that students are familiar with the assessment format and that the assessment criteria are clear and understandable.

Special attention is paid to the competence of graders and to the process for assessing to ensure it is fair and equitable. Principles 1 through 4 are supported with additional guidelines such as timely and beneficial feedback to students, accommodation for the diverse needs of students, and criteria that take into account progression for attaining academic standards.

Recent assessment principle and standards that were specifically designed for CBE are addressed in *Quality Framework for Competency-Based Education Programs* (Competency-Based Education Network [C-BEN], 2017a). The eight principles were developed by the 30 C-BEN institutions and 4 state university systems, as well as more than 100 stakeholders throughout the nation. The principle that pertains to assessment was designed specifically to address the role of assessment for CBE programs based on institutional experience and knowledge. The principle and standards from "Credential-Level Assessment Strategy With Robust Implementation" (C-BEN, 2017a) are as follows:

> PRINCIPLE: Authentic assessments and their corresponding rubrics are key components since CBE is anchored by the belief that progress toward a credential should be determined by what learners know and are able to do. The overarching assessment strategy is comprised of assessments designed both to inform the learning journey (often referred to as "assessment for learning" or formative assessment) and to validate mastery (often referred to as "assessment of learning" or summative assessment). In CBE models, assessments are intentionally aligned to competencies and cognitive levels, and use a range of assessment types and modalities to measure the transfer of learning into varied contexts and mastery of competencies. Authentic assessment design and use follows best practice for assessment professionals.

STANDARDS:

1. Authentic assessments are built within and aligned to an overarching assessment strategy for the competency being measured and the credential being earned.
2. The assessment strategy clearly articulates how the set of assessments supports the learning journey for students, matches the cognitive level of the competencies being demonstrated, and determines mastery at the appropriate academic level.
3. The set of authentic assessments is designed to provide learners with multiple opportunities and ways to demonstrate competency, including measures for both learning and ability to apply (or transfer) that learning in novel settings and situations.
4. The assessment strategy and each of the assessments and their corresponding rubrics equitably measure learning outcomes across diverse student groups, while guarding against bias in formative and summative assessment.
5. Faculty understand the faculty role in the overarching assessment strategy for the credential and are trained in and can articulate the critical role played by each assessment in validating mastery of a competency.
6. Each authentic assessment is transparently aligned to program competencies and its corresponding rubric, is

rigorous, has clear and valid measures, and is approved by faculty and assessment professionals.

7. Formative assessments serve as a tool for learning, providing feedback for reflection and refinement while also offering a feedback loop that is timely and appropriate to the competency and intent of the assessment.

8. Summative assessments' ability to measure application or the "can do" aspect of a competency is validated by a subject matter expert, ideally one external to the program design team.

9. The assessment design accommodates personalization for learners by offering flexibility in when assessments will be administered, often supported by technology.

10. The timeliness of feedback from assessments enables learners to proceed with the absolute minimum of delay. Technology is used wherever possible to facilitate and expedite the timeliness of feedback. (p. 17)

The C-BEN's (2017b) *Quality Framework for Competency-Based Education Programs* includes rubrics that would be helpful for CBE leaders in designing assessment strategies and models. The rubric lists a total of 10 criteria that align to the standards and range across 4 levels (initial, emerging, developed, highly developed). It is important to note that *Quality Framework* was written to be agnostic to CBE models, permitting institutions to vary in their approach to building a CBE program while maintaining quality. You will find it most helpful to carefully and thoughtfully review the principles, standards, and rubric in the very beginning of your program design. If your institution has already developed a CBE program, using the rubric as a self-evaluation tool may also help to identify areas for improvement.

In summary, use of these various assessment principles in your planning and revising stages as a CBE leader would prove beneficial in developing your assessment strategies.

Types and Properties

Types of Assessment

The different types of assessment are important to explore in order to secure the best alignment of a competency to its respective assessment tool. Although there are volumes of books that address the types and properties of assessment, the purpose of this section is to provide a brief guide to the types of assessment normally used in CBE programs.

Here are definitions of types of assessment commonly used in CBE programs. These definitions are adapted from *Clarifying Competency Based Education Terms* (Everhart, Sandeen, Seymour, & Yoshino, 2014).

- *Performance-based assessments* describe assignments such as presentations, papers, projects, and so on that require instructor judgment, usually through use of a rubric. The instructor applies the grading process to each student individually.
- *Objective-based assessments* describe examinations or tests, typically timed, of student learning outcomes or competencies in a format of right-and-wrong options. These tests can include multiple-choice, yes–no, true–false, fill-in-the-blank, and matching questions. The test is graded by the instructor or through technology means that evaluate responses by applying the answer key.
- *Summative assessments* refer to the use of assessment results by instructors to determine whether a student has achieved a learning outcome or competency. In CBE programs, summative assessments represent the final assessment of a specific competency. Summative assessments can be performance based or objective based.
- *Formative assessments* are diagnostic in nature and refer to the use of assessment results by instructors to improve student learning and performance. In CBE programs, formative assessments are usually considered part of the educational journey and represent another strategy for students to acquire knowledge and practice skills. Formative assessments can be performance based or objective based.
- *Authentic assessments* describe the manner and content of the assessment that is as close as possible to the way in which the competency will be demonstrated in an individual's professional and/or civic life. (pp. 8–9)

Summative assessments are similar to a final comprehensive assessment of a large unit of learning (i.e., course). In CBE, when students pass a summative assessment, it represents their mastery of a competency. It is interesting to note that the majority of summative assessments for CBE programs are performance-based assessments. For example, to demonstrate mastery in an oral communication competency, a student would prepare an outline, write a speech, and perform the speech in front of an audience. This performance-based activity would be assessed by a grader who uses a rubric.

Formative assessments (i.e., check for understanding) can be objective based, such as completing a short multiple-choice quiz following study of a specific content area, or can be performance based, such as providing a basic outline for a paper or a first section of a portfolio. Some institutions "match" the types of formative and summative assessments so they are both objective based or both performance based. However, there is no right or wrong way, and the institution will need to determine the best approach to ensure student success.

In addition, authentic assessments are emphasized in summative assessment approaches to ensure a stronger link between what learners know and can do and what is expected when they are employed in the field. For example, to obtain a CBE business degree, students will likely write and present a business plan to ensure they are prepared for what will be required of them on the job.

Performance-based assessments in competency-based programs are most often locally designed (homegrown) by faculty who create assignments and rubrics for evaluating student work. Objective-based assessments can also be locally designed by faculty who write test items and/or select and adapt items from test banks.

Another type of assessment used in competency-based programs are standardized assessments.

- *Standardized assessments* describe a test that is administered in the same way for all test takers (i.e., all test takers answer the same questions or a selection of questions from a common bank of questions) and is scored in the same consistent manner. Standardized tests are usually norm referenced in that an individual's score can be compared to others in a predefined population.

In CBE programs, standardized assessments may be present in programs that align with professional standards or industry-specific careers. For example, a CBE bachelor of science in information technology program may include industry-accepted certification examinations such as CompTIA A+, CompTIA Cloud+, and MTA Software Development Fundamentals. When students pass these standardized certification examinations, they represent an accepted understanding of mastery of learning (i.e., competency).

Properties of Assessment

Whether an assessment is locally developed or commercially prepared, an institution will need to answer the following questions:

1. Is this assessment tool reliable? Is the tool consistent?
2. Is this assessment tool valid? Does the tool assess what it purports to measure?

The two main properties of assessment address the consistency of an assessment tool (reliability) and the "fit" of the tool for the topics assessed (validity). Maki (2010) described these properties as follows:

- *Reliability* refers to how well a measurement fairly or consistently assesses the expected traits or dimensions of student learning. It also measures how consistently scorers or scoring systems grade student responses.
- *Interrater reliability* is the degree to which different graders or observers agree in their scoring.
- *Validity* refers to how accurately an assessment corresponds to what is being tested. *Validity* is defined as the extent to which an assessment accurately measures what it is intended to measure.

In CBE, properties of reliability and validity are essential to adequately address the defensibility of the program. Students' progression through a program and attainment of the credential is based on their mastery of summative assessments. Institutions must be able to defend their assessments, showing evidence of reliability and validity.

If an institution is using performance-based assessments with locally developed rubrics and scoring criteria, it will need to answer the question: "Is this assessment reliable (consistent)?" Institutions can address reliability by training and calibrating graders initially, having more than one independent grader, and keeping data on consistency of scoring across graders. A threshold agreement level (i.e., 90%) can be set with a third individual being asked to grade should there be low interrater agreement.

To ensure validity for locally developed assessment tools (performance based or objective based), experts can evaluate the "match" of the assessment tool to the content assessed. Faculty subject matter experts and students can also participate in this exercise to help to determine face validity. Maki (2010) suggested, "The discussions that surround learning outcome statements, curricular and co-curricular design, pedagogy, models of teaching and learning, and philosophies of teaching provide the necessary institution- and program-level context within which to analyze the validity of methods" (p. 163).

Program Assessment Project Plan

Once the competency statements and supporting objectives are written, the institution can start planning the creation of summative assessments. This project plan will assist CBE leaders in getting the right talent around the table, address significant questions regarding the institutional approach to summative assessments, and develop a project plan with timelines.

Table 3.1 presents a CBE program assessment project plan that details decisions to be made and assignments. We will walk through each of these columns (or buckets of information). Please note that you may wish to add or delete sections that may not align with your institutional approach.

1. *Competency statement and objectives (column 1).* List the complete competency statement and the supporting objectives in column 1. In thinking through your institution's approach to summative assessment, you may wish to consider the following:

TABLE 3.1
Competency-Based Education Program Assessment Project Plan

Competency Statement and Objectives	Summative Assessment Type (Project Based or Objective Based)	Summative Assignment	Faculty or Subject Matter Expert	Other Staff	Approval Process	Timeline and Due Date	Alternative Forms

      a. Will each competency have its own (unique) summative assessment?

      b. If yes, list all competencies and objectives individually.

      c. If no, you will need to group the competencies together that will be combined for one summative assessment.

2. *Summative assessment type (column 2).* Determine if the summative assessment will be performance based or objective based. To help you make this decision, you may wish to discuss the level of learning according to Bloom's taxonomy.

      a. How will you know if students have mastered this competency? How can they demonstrate their learning?

      b. What is the level of learning in the competency? The verb used in the statement will help to determine the level of learning. Lower Bloom taxonomies use verbs of *remember* and *understand,* which may indicate that objective-based assessment would be appropriate. Higher Bloom taxonomies use verbs of *apply, analyze, evaluate,* and *create.* These verbs may point you in the direction of performance-based assessment.

      c. Does your institution wish to use all performance-based assessments regardless of levels of learning?

      d. Do standardized or certification examinations exist that align with specific competencies?

3. *Summative assignment (column 3).* Determine the assignment for performance-based assessments and write a brief description. For objective-based assessments, you can list multiple-choice exams, matching, and so on.

      a. For performance-based assessments, write a full description of what students must demonstrate and do that represents evidence of the competency.

      b. For performance-based assessments, does the description of the assignment include all of the objectives? Is the description clear and comprehensive?

4. *Faculty or subject matter expert (column 4).* List the faculty or subject matter expert assigned to the competency. Institutions may recruit faculty and/or ask for volunteers. Faculty buy-in is critical for this work, and it is strongly recommended that this work not be one more thing on the

plate. Many institutions adjust faculty workloads and/or provide additional compensation.

   a. Do you have the needed talent and expertise for all competencies? Do you need to seek additional faculty or subject matter experts?
   b. Are there too many competencies assigned to one person?
   c. Will this faculty member or subject matter expert be responsible for creating the summative assignment and assessment only? Will this faculty member or subject matter expert be responsible for the later step of curriculum, learning activities, and formative assessment?

5. *Other staff (column 5).* Indicate if other staff are needed for the program assessment project plan.

   a. Will the faculty member or subject matter expert need training and/or assistance in creating the summative assessments? If so, who will provide the help? Some institutions have hired (full-time or consultant) competency-based assessment experts to work with faculty, whereas others rely on institutional assessment office staff and/or assessment leaders in the institution.
   b. Does your institution have a center for teaching and learning that can assist with creation of summative assessments?

6. *Approval process (column 6).* Determine the approval process for summative assessments. How assessments are vetted and approved will help set reasonable expectations for roles and responsibilities, as well as timelines and due dates.

   a. Is there an assessment committee that will approve the assessments?
   b. Is there a faculty curriculum team that will approve the assessments?
   c. Will an institutional assessment expert approve the assessments?
   d. Will the assessments be vetted with employers or advisory groups?

7. *Timeline and due date (column 7).* Work closely with the faculty member or subject matter expert in determining due dates. Dependent on the number of competencies and

sequencing of competencies in a student's program, this work can be phased across time.

   a. What is the final date for all of the work to be completed? On the basis of this date, the work can be divided across time.

   b. Do some faculty and subject matter experts have more than one competency? If so, due dates will also need to be spread out.

8. *Alternative forms (column 8).* Objective-based assessments will need more than one form of the assessment if students are permitted to retake the exam. Building alternative forms will need to be integrated into the timeline. Some institutions also develop different scenarios or assignments for performance-based assessments, which would also require additional versions.

   a. Will students be permitted to retake failed attempts for objective-based assessments? If yes, how many failed attempts? Number of attempts will guide the institution in knowing how many alternative forms are needed.

   b. Does the institution wish to have more than one scenario or assignment for performance-based assessments? If yes, the institution will need to develop additional summative assignments and determine whether the same assessment tool (rubric) can be used for various assignments.

Conclusion

As the institutional leader of CBE, you will find it is important to work closely with your assessment experts. In this way, the leap from assessment practices in the credit-hour program to assessment in CBE will likely be a smoother transition. Gathering a team of assessment and curriculum experts will ensure the building of quality programs and defensible assessment models and strategies.

4

THE LEARNING
JOURNEY

In competency-based learning models, it is incumbent on academic leaders to create an environment where learners can succeed by demonstrating the required collection of competencies. Institutions, often inadvertently, create barriers to success through decisions, processes, and systems that do not have the best interests of the learner in mind. Institutions must comprehensively understand the strengths and needs of the targeted learner population so these students are well served by the competency-based education (CBE) program. Although the student life cycle should be evaluated, from first point of contact through to graduation and alumni relations, to ensure the student experience is being designed holistically, this chapter will focus on the learning journey—the part of the student life cycle under the purview of academic affairs. This journey should include determining learner's fit with program, sharing policies and procedures, designing wraparound student support services, moving the learner to competence, providing a robust learning environment, and creating a sense of community.

Determining Learner–Program Fit

Depending on the design of an institution's CBE program, it may be beneficial to the learner and the institution to determine if the match between individual and pedagogy is solid. There is a wide range of approaches used by CBE institutions to determine fit, including personalized interviews, preenrollment assessments, and preview classes. Although the topic of student orientation and fit were discussed in chapter 2, "Program Design," it is important to consider this first step of the educational journey. For this purpose, we will take another look at determining the learner–program fit.

For institutions using personalized interviews, the following questions are good to ask. It is important that personalized interviews include a time for learners to ask questions of the institution's representatives too.

- Why are you interested in pursuing this credential?
- What are your academic and career goals?
- What is your ideal learning environment?
- What is your level of competence with technology?
- What types of support do you anticipate needing as you seek your credential?
- What will keep you motivated to finish your credential?
- What is your timeline for completing this program?

Some institutions, and even a few vendors, have created preenrollment assessments to determine learner–program fit. These assessments are based on the institution's CBE model, typically asking specific questions about program features and the learner's appreciation or aptitude for each feature. For example, the learner would be asked to indicate agreement on the following statements. If the learner responds positively to the program's features, the CBE program is deemed to be a good fit.

- I prefer a highly structured learning environment.
- I prefer an environment where I have deadlines set for me.
- I prefer to work independently, seeking assistance when needed.
- I prefer to choose the order of my classes and the sequencing of content I am learning.
- I prefer face-to-face interactions with my fellow classmates.
- I prefer to have the accountability of a weekly check-in call with my faculty.

Many CBE programs offer prospective and new students a realistic preview of the program so both the student and the institution have confidence in the match between learners and pedagogy. Some institutions require students to take a free orientation course and demonstrate their competence in CBE before allowing them to register in official course work. Others create a low-risk first course that embeds all of the features of the CBE program so learners get exposed to all of the model's elements right away. This allows learners to experience the competency-based approach, use the enabling technology, and identify whether they can be successful in the format.

Sharing Policies and Procedures

CBE programs should communicate expectations clearly, especially related to the institutional policies, structure, and expectations of the program. This information must include information on tuition, fees, and the availability of financial aid. These policies and procedures should be written in plain language and avoid the use of jargon and acronyms. An institution's expectations may be shared simply as a one-page document, which is reviewed with learners each semester. Some institutions go a step further and ask learners to sign a statement saying they were made aware of the policies, structure, and program expectations. This is the ideal time to determine the expectations learners have of the institution and its staff. For other institutions, the inclusion of policies and procedures in the student handbook and course syllabi is the chosen approach.

Institutions may also choose to put additional information in writing. For example, at Lipscomb University, learners enter into a coaching contract with their assigned faculty coach. Figure 4.1 shows Lipscomb's learner–faculty coach contract.

The learner and the faculty-coach are asked to identify what they expect of each other, such as the frequency of meetings, assessment requirements, and grading. The contract governs their relationship and ensures there is no confusion between the two. Although Lipscomb's contracts vary from learner to learner, the basic format is consistent across all learners.

Figure 4.1. Competency development coaching agreement.

Competency Development Coaching Agreement

Coach: [Coach Name]

Student: [Student Name]

Coaching will begin on <u>01/05/2018</u> and will end <u>04/24/2018</u> to 04/30/18

Final competency assessment will take place by: <u>04/03/2018</u>

This assessment will be in the form of: <u>Relationship Building will be assessed via an observed group activity (or activities) lasting approximately 45 to 90 minutes in total.</u>

Student Understandings

- I understand I will be assigned skill development apps in myCompass (powered by Fidelis), which have been carefully created to help foster the competency that was identified as a development area in the assessment center. While this work is optional, it is extremely important to reaching the student goal of strong competency.
- I understand that leadership competencies take time and internal work to develop. It may take two or more semesters of hard work to develop a competency, or it may go very rapidly. Course progress is up to my willingness to be honest, introspective, and proactive in my work on myCompass, behavior change, and with my coach.
- To pass this course, I understand that I must demonstrate this competency in an authentic assessment (in a center or other observed activity as agreed on by the College of Professional Studies [CoPS], noted previously) as assessed by a trained behavioral assessor (not my coach). Simply doing the work will not gain credit. I must develop the competency to the level that I can apply it in an authentic work or simulated work setting.
- I understand that if I do not pass the assessment at the end of the first semester, I will get an IP (in progress grade) and continue to work with my coach for the following semester. If I do not pass the assessment at that time, I will be assigned a different coach and will have to re-enroll in the course.
- I understand that my coach believes that I can develop this competency, and he/she and the academic team will support my own efforts in that development.

(Continues)

Figure 4.1. (*Continued*)

- CONFIDENTIALITY: I understand that the content of my conversations with my coach are confidential, and the content will be shared only with the CoPS academic team (other coaches and coach support) for the purpose of improving the coaching experience. The CoPS academic team is bound by confidentiality as well. The exception to the confidentiality agreement is when information is revealed that might cause harm to myself or others.

The Work Plan

- The work plan will be created by the coach and student and will be finalized by 01/16/2018. This plan will include the learning apps that the student will be assigned, the coaching relationship, finding and interacting with a mentor, and other learning experiences the student and coach may agree on.
- The coach will reflect weekly on the work plan. This reflection will be shared with the coach's coach and/or the COPS academic team.
- Coach and student will review our work plan **midway** through our work together by 03/13/2018. The coach will write a reflection on this work and will share it with the CoPS academic team.
- Coach and student will reflect on our work plan at the **end** of our designated time together. The coach will write a reflection on this work and will share it with the CoPS academic team. This will occur immediately before the final behavioral assessment.

Meeting Logistics

- We will meet for a minimum of 8 to 10 sessions (20–30 minutes) per semester.
- Our meetings will take place on Wednesdays, from 3:30 p.m. to 4:00 p.m.
- The location for our meetings will be via telephone (on campus if needed).
- Our time will be documented on the coaching log, which can be shared with the COPS or kept on an online platform that the CoPS academic team can view.
- If one of us has to cancel a meeting, whenever possible we will give the other person at least 24 hours' notice. We also recognize that unexpected things come up and that sometimes we are forced to cancel without notice.

(*Continues*)

Figure 4.1. (*Continued*)

- If the coach cancels a meeting, he or she will make every possible effort to reschedule as soon as possible.
- If the student cancels a meeting, the coach will make an effort to reschedule, but cannot always promise that this will happen due to his or her other commitments.
- If cancelations become a pattern, the coach and student agree to review the coaching agreement.

Feedback
- The coach welcomes feedback from the student at any time. The student is encouraged to share feedback.
- The coach will ask the student for formal feedback **midway** through the coaching contract by 03/13/2018 and at the end of working together.

We agree to work together under the previously-described conditions. We understand that doing so will increase the likelihood of developing the competency of Relationship Building.

Coach signature:

Date:

Student signature:

Date:

Designing Wraparound Student Support Services

Competency-based learning focuses on helping learners master needed competencies. Students frequently encounter challenges as they seek to complete college and demonstrate their competence. Oft-cited reasons for noncompletion include cost, work–life demands, lack of proper planning, failure to become connected, and courses that did not count toward degree requirements because of transferring or delayed major declarations.

CBE programs offer some combination of services that wrap around the learner to support the individual throughout the learning journey. The wraparound services and supports provided vary by institution but could include the following:

- Individualized coaching
- Career counseling
- Financial counseling
- Psychological counseling
- Mentorship
- Technology assistance, including provision of computers
- Child care and elder care assistance
- Financial aid assistance, including emergency funds for tuition shortages
- Scholarships for books, materials, and learning resources
- Community service and engagement opportunities
- Housing support
- Legal services
- Tax assistance
- 24/7 or modified institutional service hours

CBE programs integrate regular and frequent communication from the institution to the learner so at-risk students can be identified. Also, through the use of predictive analytics featured in many CBE learning platforms, faculty and staff can be alerted to behaviors that deviate from anticipated performance. For example, if a student has not scheduled a check-in call with his or her coach, the coach will be notified so the coach can proactively reach out to the student.

CBE institutions invest in deeply understanding the learners to be served by its CBE program (Competency-Based Education Network, 2017a). By knowing their learners, these institutions can determine the challenges most likely to be barriers to completion and design student support services to assist learners with their degree persistence. There are multiple ways institutional leaders can seek to know and understand their target students, including by

- reading current literature on this topic,
- reviewing surveys completed by existing students with a similar profile as the target students,

- interviewing current and prospective students, and
- conducting focus groups of prospective students.

Although there is not a substantial amount of research specific to CBE, there are many studies on the needs of various student populations. An institution should not rely on this information alone when determining its wraparound support services. Existing students could be surveyed to determine their needs, identify gaps in services, and generate suggestions for improvement. If possible, surveys of previous students—including those who did not persist to graduation—could be administered to gain a fuller perspective. As an alternative to surveys, interviews and focus groups could be held to solicit similar information. In addition, by conducting focus groups with prospective students, institutions can get clarity on the most important wraparound student support services to the specific students the institution hopes to attract.

Moving the Learner Toward Competence

Once the credential's competencies have been fully identified and what constitutes a successful demonstration of those competencies has been determined, you can begin crafting the learning journey. This timing follows the backward design process described in earlier chapters. During this stage of CBE program development, you are answering the following question: "How will our program move learners from where they are today to the point of demonstrating mastery of this competency?"

To answer this question, you should begin with your competency statements and your summative assessments. For example, assume one of your program's competencies is "I can deliver effective oral presentations." To demonstrate this competency, the learner will need to exhibit mastery by organizing and publicly delivering both informative and persuasive presentations that effectively incorporate technology and audience participation.

Next, create a list of knowledge, skills, abilities, and intellectual behaviors needed to demonstrate mastery. To demonstrate this competency, the learner will need to acquire the knowledge, skills and abilities, and intellectual behaviors shown in Table 4.1.

TABLE 4.1
Knowledge, Skills and Abilities, and Intellectual Behaviors

Knowledge	Skills and Abilities	Intellectual Behaviors
• Communication theory • Presentation methods • Presentation format • Storytelling strategies	• Organization and flow of content • Use of vocal inflection • Use of eye contact • Ability to diffuse hostility in questions	• Composure • Confidence • Rapport building • Diplomacy

Once this list has been completed and validated by internal and external subject matter experts, faculty can begin to curate materials to teach this information. In CBE programs, the curation of content should not be left to the student. Students should not be left to learn on their own. Instead, learning materials are carefully and thoughtfully selected for learners' use.

To reduce costs, many CBE institutions choose to curate *open educational resources* so institutions and students can access learning materials at no charge. Others create their own digital collection of material, of which some may be licensed content at a minimal fee. For some institutions, partnering with a vendor to curate and deliver learning content is the best way to meet the institution's and learners' needs.

With the educational reading materials selected, the learning journey is enhanced with activities, assignments, and formative assessments. These learning activities should be created for and aligned to the competencies and summative assessments. This alignment should be transparent to students to reduce resistance and increase the likelihood of completion. Like with assessments, learning activities should be meaningful and authentic. This means it should be evident to learners how the activity or assignment will help them personally or professionally. When possible, learning activities should mirror tasks learners might be asked to complete in their desired career.

Table 4.2 illustrates how the learning journey could be crafted for the "I can deliver effective oral presentations" competency.

TABLE 4.2
Learning Journey for the "I Can Deliver Effective Oral Presentations" Competency

Knowledge, Skills and Abilities, Intellectual Behaviors	Proposed Activity, Assignment, Formative Assessment
Communication theory	• *Assignment:* Read curated materials. • *Assignment:* Complete worksheet designed to illustrate the root cause of well-known communication failures. • *Assignment:* Watch a series of videos with examples and nonexamples of effective communication, properly identifying the underlying theory illustrated. • *Assessment:* Complete an objective-style test over the theory and key concepts.
Vocal inflection	• *Assignment:* Read curated materials. • *Activity:* Deliver five 1-minute impromptu presentations on a wide range of topics, each designed to require different vocal inflections. • *Assignment:* Watch a video recording of two famous speeches, identifying when and how the presenter used vocal inflection effectively.
Composure	• *Assignment:* Read curated materials. • *Assignment:* Watch two different presidential press secretaries during a daily briefing, identifying the strategies they used to maintain or regain composure. • *Activity:* Select a polarizing issue in the United States today, make a persuasive public presentation advocating for one side of the issue, and then field audience questions.

The following list illustrates a range of potential learning activities that could be used in CBE programs (EDUCAUSE, 2005):

- Authentic project
- Behavioral modeling

- Brainstorming
- Case studies
- Cognitive modeling
- Concept mapping
- Debate
- Discussion
- Drill and practice
- Essay
- Experiment
- Field trip
- Game
- Interview
- Journaling
- Literature review
- Peer exchange
- Performance modeling
- Presentation
- Scavenger hunt
- Service-learning
- Simulation
- Socratic instruction
- Test
- Working session

Regardless of the chosen activity, learners should be given timely and constructive feedback from faculty on their submissions. Students should be provided with the opportunity to revise submissions based on this feedback so they can achieve mastery of the assignment.

Providing a Robust Learning Environment

CBE programs provide students with a robust learning environment. Although learning environments vary by institution, academic model, and the needs of learners, highly effective learning environments share common characteristics (Heick, 2014).

1. CBE programs should create a safe place for learners to ask questions. A curious learner is more likely to engage and internalize the learning (Heick, 2014).

2. CBE programs should ensure ideas come from divergent sources. Learning activities should come from a variety of sources, such as employers, professional and cultural mentors, peers, community members, and content experts outside of higher education (Heick, 2014).

3. CBE programs should use a variety of learning methods. Quality programs coherently blend diverse methods of teaching, including inquiry-based learning, project-based learning, direct instruction, peer-to-peer learning, employer-based learning, mobile learning, flipped classroom, and many others (Heick, 2014).

4. CBE programs connect to a larger community. Learning in the classroom makes sense in the real world and often addresses specific community needs. Institutions integrate meaningful opportunities for students to engage with employers and build networking connections (Heick, 2014).

5. CBE programs personalize learning by a variety of criteria. Learners have the opportunity to customize their learning journey based on their individual needs and interests. Institutions clearly communicate what portions of the learning journey can be personalized by learners (Heick, 2014).

6. CBE programs make the criteria for success transparent to learners. Students should never have to guess what it takes to be successful. Competencies and the required demonstration for achieving mastery should be openly shared with students (Heick, 2014).

7. CBE programs use technology to enable learning. Although CBE programs do not have to be offered online, programs should leverage technology across the student life cycle (Competency-Based Education Network, 2017a).

8. CBE programs are sufficiently resourced, with the appropriate levels and types of faculty and staff. The roles of faculty and staff are differentiated and clearly defined. Learners know whom to call for what they need (Competency-Based Education Network, 2017a).

9. CBE programs monitor the performance of all involved. Faculty and staff monitor learners to ensure the students are fully informed, engaged, and performing as anticipated.

Faculty and staff performance is monitored against a similar set of performance metrics. Performance gaps are rapidly addressed, and exemplary performance is rewarded (Competency-Based Education Network, 2017a).

10. CBE programs support learners regardless of race, ethnicity, economic status, or ability. This includes evaluating the learning journey to ensure no decision, process, or system negatively affects underserved or underrepresented learners (Competency-Based Education Network, 2017a).

Creating a Sense of Community

Learners, faculty, staff, and other stakeholders of a CBE program enjoy a sense of community based on their shared commitment to create more competent graduates. This commitment leads to deeper, more authentic relationships and a feeling that all members matter to one another. For example, CBE program staff get to know and often share an emotional connection with the learners. The staff know the role they play in helping learners succeed in their learning journey. Furthermore, staff know they have the ability to influence the learners' outcome in the program. When students succeed, staff feel rewarded for their participation in making this success possible. Similar statements could be made of faculty, employers, peers, and the learners themselves. This community helps to ensure the needs of learners are met, and in return, this should yield better outcomes than those in non-CBE environments.

Conclusion

In conclusion, CBE programs carefully craft the learning journey so students are able to master the required competencies as efficiently and effectively as possible. This journey is based on learner fit with the program's design, transparent sharing policies and procedures, wraparound student support services, deliberately moving the learner to competence, a robust learning environment, and a sense of community among all those involved in the academic process.

5

FACULTY AND
STAFF MODELS AND
CONSIDERATIONS

Institutions have modified, enhanced, and created various faculty and staff models in competency-based education (CBE) programs to support learning and student success. A review of institutions that offer CBE programs will reveal a wide variety of positions and job titles such as tutorial faculty, faculty mentors, coaches, advisers, mentors, faculty coaches, part-time faculty, traditional faculty, and subject matter experts.

To add to this richness of positions (or confusion), job titles and positions do not universally reflect similar roles and responsibilities. What a *faculty mentor* does at one institution may be what a *coach* performs at another institution. Likewise, an *adviser* at an institution may perform similar duties of what a *coach* does at another institution.

It is necessary to conduct a deeper probe that asks specifically what a person does on the job to fully grasp the roles and responsibilities to support CBE. There are also many other key staff positions that provide services and support for CBE, including instructional designers and personnel from the offices of admissions, registrar, financial aid, outreach, marketing, and business.

As a leader of CBE, you will find that consideration of these roles and responsibilities for faculty and staff will assist you in determining the best-suited models for your institution. In this chapter, we will explore the faculty and staff models and considerations with a closer look at the specific roles and responsibilities:

- Faculty
- Coach
- Student support and services staff
- Considerations for building faculty and staff models

Faculty

There are numerous definitions with varying roles and responsibilities for the terms *faculty* and *faculty member*. However, there is a common understanding that even with a wide range of responsibilities, faculty are educators, academics, and teachers. Many institutions have faculty ranks such as assistant professor, associate professor, and professor, as well as instructor, lecturer, and adjunct faculty. Threaded in these titles, what are the specific roles and responsibilities for faculty serving CBE programs? The answer? It depends.

Everhart, Sandeen, Seymour, and Yoshino (2014) cited, "Faculty in competency-based education programs are responsible for one or more of the following tasks: subject matter expert, curriculum design, assignment development, assessment/grading, mentoring, advisement, and/or coaching" (p. 15). One can see through this broad brushstroke definition that faculty are key throughout the CBE program from its creation, design, assessment, grading, and advising.

The Competency-Based Education Network (C-BEN) conducted a survey of its member organizations to better understand how faculty and staff roles differ across institutions offering CBE programs. Initially in this survey, the 30 colleges and universities and 4 public university systems that comprise C-BEN membership were asked about job positions and titles that serve their respective CBE programs. But that created even more misunderstandings, as titles did not uniformly provide agreed-on roles and responsibilities across institutions. To help clarify the roles and responsibilities, the survey then asked what were the specific roles and responsibilities in the functional areas of curriculum, assessment, instruction, and coaching, advising, and mentoring (Cleary et al., 2015).

The C-BEN survey results, definitions of *faculty serving competency-based programs*, and institutional case studies will serve as the starting point for discussing these countless roles and responsibilities within each of these functional areas.

Program Development and Curriculum

A primary role and responsibility of faculty is creating the CBE program and developing the curriculum. This role is similar to what faculty do in credit-hour programs. Exploring these key areas will assist with identifying needs, clarifying roles and responsibilities, and developing job descriptions. As much as possible, these functions will represent many different institutional models of CBE in hopes to be model agnostic. Some of these roles and responsibilities may fit and be well aligned with those of current institutional faculty positions, whereas some may not. Adapted and adopted from the C-BEN survey (Cleary et al., 2015) is a list of common roles and responsibilities for faculty in the functional areas of program development and curriculum, shown in Figure 5.1.

In reviewing the list of responsibilities for faculty, you might find it helpful to think about what current roles and duties the faculty at your institution are responsible for. Do these CBE-related responsibilities align with the roles and responsibilities of your faculty? What is missing? After you determine what additional roles and responsibilities are needed, it may be helpful for you to then discuss with your faculty the best way to address the needs of developing a CBE program and creating the curriculum.

Assessment

What are the key roles and functions that faculty play in assessments for CBE programs? As we discovered in chapter 3, there are two major types of assessments in CBE programs. Formative assessment is the first type that learners encounter, and as we learned, formative assessment is embedded in the learning activities. Formative assessment normally occurs after a learner has engaged with academic content and then is asked to complete a quiz or submit a draft of a project or writing assignment (e.g., outline, rough draft). The second type of assessment is summative assessment, which represents mastery of a competency. The summative assessment may require a final project, examination, written report, and so on.

Assessments are the keystone to a CBE program as part of the learning activities and to ensure mastery of learning. As part of the learning journey, assessments gauge what learners know and what they need to continue to work on. In some programs, especially in

Figure 5.1. Faculty responsibilities: Program development and curriculum.

Program Development

1. Determine pedagogical approach to CBE program
2. Write competency statements and objectives
3. Write learning objectives for each competency
4. Ensure alignment of learning objectives to competency
5. Categorize competencies into domains and subdomains
6. Scaffold and sequence competencies for program completion
7. Crosswalk competencies to credit hour (required by regional accreditors and U.S. Department of Education)
8. Develop policies and processes for curriculum and assessment development and approval

Curriculum

1. Provide content expertise for developing learning resources
2. Provide content expertise for creating learning activities
3. Align learning resources and content to learning objectives
4. Align learning activities to learning objectives
5. Provide content expertise for adaptive learning
6. Ensure appropriate level of learning for program level
7. Ensure alignment of content to performance standards
8. Create curriculum maps
9. Develop opportunities for field-related learning experiences such as internships, practicum, clinical
10. Create opportunities for peer, employer, and/or stakeholder interaction
11. Serve as quality manager with oversight of competency
12. Develop evidence-based continuous improvement process for competency

Note. Adapted from *Faculty and Staff Roles and Responsibilities in the Design and Delivery of Competency-Based Programs: A C-BEN Snapshot*, by Cleary et al., 2015, December, Competency-Based Education Network. Retrieved from www.cbenetwork.org/resource-library/?category=141246

online CBE programs, formative assessments provide the data for adaptive learning engines that guide students through an intentionally designed learning journey based on evidence of knowledge. Through backward design, assessment creation occurs prior to curriculum development, further emphasizing the importance and "front and center" status of assessment in CBE design.

So what are the specific roles and responsibilities of faculty in assessment? Figure 5.2 provides a list of assessment-related functions for faculty, adopted and adapted from the C-BEN survey (Cleary et al., 2015), categorized in the areas of formative assessments, summative assessments, and grading.

As you can see, the assessment responsibilities for faculty are broad and deep. From the assessment creation function, faculty must be well versed in item development, item selection, and rubric development. As a grader, faculty are required to use rubrics to evaluate assignments. An important aspect of grading is calibration across graders to ensure reliable scoring. Faculty's expertise and interest may cut across most of the assessment-related tasks. However, this may vary among faculty, with some being comfortable with all aspects of assessment and some not feeling confident with assessment in general. Some universities hire faculty with assessment expertise to fulfill this role, and others have hired psychometricians to collaborate with faculty in developing assessments.

As a CBE leader, you will need to determine faculty's expertise and interest in assessment and provide resources to support faculty in understanding how this critically important aspect functions when creating quality CBE programs.

Instruction

What does the term *instruction* mean for CBE programs? If one asked faculty serving CBE programs, how would they describe their teaching? Broadly known is that instruction is to educate, give guidance, and disseminate information in a content area. For CBE programs, we can expand this definition to include qualified experts giving advice, providing academic support, and helping learners achieve learning goals.

Solér (2016), director of CBE and assessment at the University of North Carolina, stated,

> Competency-based pedagogy does not mean there's a single multiple-choice, standardized test that indicates competency or provides a degree. Rather, this rigorous academic, problem-based pedagogy and student-focused program delivery strategy weaves competencies throughout the curriculum and supports students where they need it most.

Figure 5.2. Faculty responsibilities: Assessment.

Formative Assessment Creation 1. Develop pretest (if applicable) through faculty generation of items or selection of items from test bank 2. Develop formative assessments through faculty generation of items, selection of items from test bank, and/or assignment throughout educational journey 3. Ensure alignment of pretest to learning objectives and competency 4. Ensure alignment of formative assessment to learning objectives and competency 5. Create alternative test forms if needed 6. Ensure accuracy of formative assessments 7. Serve as quality manager of formative assessments

Summative Assessment Creation
  1. Develop assignment for performance-based summative assessment
  2. Ensure clarity of assignment for performance-based summative assessment
  3. Align assignment to learning objectives for performance-based summative assessment
  4. Develop objective-based summative assessment through faculty generation of items and/or selection of items from test bank
  5. Ensure alignment of learning objectives with standardized examinations (if applicable)
  6. Develop assessment criteria and rubrics for performance-based assessment
  7. Ensure reliability (i.e., intergrader) and validity for performance-based summative assessment
  8. Ensure reliability and validity for objective-based summative assessment
  9. Create alternative test forms if needed
10. Create alternative assignments if needed
11. Ensure accuracy of test forms
12. Serve as quality manager of summative assessments and/or collaborate with assessment director

Grading 1. Evaluate formative assignment and provide feedback to students for performance-based assessments 2. Grade summative assignment and provide feedback to students for performance-based assessments

(Continues)

Figure 5.2 (*Continued*)

> 3. Participate in training and calibration in grading assignments using rubrics
> 4. Make recommendations for improving assessment tools
> 5. Ensure fairness and equity in grading

Note. Adapted from *Faculty and Staff Roles and Responsibilities in the Design and Delivery of Competency-Based Programs: A C-BEN Snapshot*, by Cleary et al., 2015, December, Competency-Based Education Network. Retrieved from www.cbenetwork.org/resource-library/?category=141246

> From the faculty perspective, teaching through competencies should not be new, but rather a much more student-friendly way of learning that is not contingent upon an institution's academic calendar, but on a student's lived experience as a working adult, a parent, a caregiver, or a combination of all of these and many others. (p. 2)

I would add a friendly amendment to the last statement by Solér in that CBE programs are not just for working adults. Although this modern version of CBE that has emerged over the past five years has focused on adult learners, there are several universities building programs for traditional-aged students. In addition, there are high school CBE programs whose graduates are seeking postsecondary degrees through a CBE delivery model.

Instructional roles and responsibilities for faculty in CBE programs vary across institutional models. See Figure 5.3 for a listing of instructional roles and responsibilities for faculty. This specific list of instructional functions of faculty can help facilitate dialogue with faculty to determine the best faculty model for their institution.

As Solér noted, many of the responsibilities listed are aligned with what faculty are currently engaged in with credit-hour programs. This may be especially true for online delivery of courses. One difference in the way faculty engage students in learning is the use of technology through adaptive learning engines, a feature of some CBE online programs. Through technology, adaptive learning algorithms rely on formative assessment results to automatically and efficiently guide learners through the material, stepping by topics and concepts already mastered and directing to areas not yet mastered or new topics and concepts.

Figure 5.3. Faculty responsibilities: Instruction.

Instructional Activities
1. Provide feedback and instruction to students on assignments.
2. Provide additional and customized instruction as needed.
3. Proactively contact students regarding academic content on a regular basis.
4. Provide substantive interaction with students on academic-related content areas.
5. Provide open office hours for learner questions and to provide academic assistance.
6. Facilitate peer interaction for instructional purposes.
7. Facilitate employer and/or discipline expert interaction for instructional purposes.
8. Collaborate with other support services such as writing centers to meet student needs.
9. Utilize technology-based tools for enhancing instruction and meeting student learning needs.

Another difference is the removal of time and schedule for pacing and the focus on learning through achievement of mastery of a competency. A faculty member in a competency-based program is following the students' pace of learning and providing assistance when needed, as well as engaging in substantive interaction with learners on a regular basis. In a credit-hour, time-based approach, if students struggle with some content in week four, they still need to keep the pace going forward with material presented in week five. In a competency-based approach, if students struggle in a specific content area, they can continue to work with the content and faculty member until they have learned enough to move forward. Students set the pace and schedule in a competency-based program. In this manner, all students in a CBE program must achieve mastery of each competency in an educational environment where time varies across students and learning is held constant.

Unbundled and Reassembled Faculty Model Considerations

A common term affiliated with CBE programs is the *unbundled faculty model*. In the previous section, we explored the many roles and responsibilities of faculty in a competency-based program of curriculum development, assessment creation, grading, and instruction. In the credit-hour program, a faculty member may be responsible for all of these key functions. In a competency-based program, faculty roles and responsibilities may be unbundled or what I like to call "reassembled." This reassembled faculty model in competency-based programs divides specific functions across faculty and staff. Both the credit-hour and the CBE approaches are built to ensure that students are getting the support they need from faculty and that faculty are provided adequate time to work with students.

An example of an unbundled and reassembled faculty model is the CBE programs at the University System of Georgia. Students enrolled in CBE programs are supported through the following key roles: (a) an *instructional strategist*, who is a generalist in the discipline and provides tutoring; (b) a *subject matter expert*, who is responsible for the design, development, and assessment of competencies; and (c) a *success coach*, who monitors student progress through the learning management system and reaches out directly to the student or contacts the instructional strategist for assistance. Each of these roles is served by different individuals who specialize in their jobs to support students.

Another example of an unbundled and reassembled faculty model is the City University of Seattle, whose faculty serving the competency-based program take on more of a coach or facilitator of learning role (Council for Adult and Experiential Learning, 2015). The City University of Seattle uses two faculty members per learning block to perform the following distinct roles: (a) *facilitators*, who provide support to learners as they progress and provide periodic guidance and feedback, and (b) *assessors*, who are responsible for assessing student submissions and evaluate students' mastery using rubrics. This division of labor between instructors and graders is frequently used in competency-based programs.

Although one will commonly see unbundled and reassembled faculty models for competency-based programs, it is not always the case. An institution may determine that the faculty serving competency-based programs engage in program and curriculum design, creation of assessments, teaching, and grading. As a CBE leader, you will find it important to honor the institutional culture, faculty, and student needs in determining the best faculty model. Before you make that decision, let's walk through the role of a coach in CBE programs.

Coach

The roles and responsibilities of a coach, a success coach, and an adviser are critical for student success in a CBE program. Everhart and colleagues (2014) cited the following: (a) Coaches "maintain an advisory relationship with a student, typically throughout the student's enrollment in a competency based education program. Coaches may also be called 'mentors' or 'student success coaches'" (p. 8); (b) advisers "provide students with guidance to make decisions in their curricular and career pathways" (p. 15); and (c) mentors "guide students through their educational processes and may also be called 'coaches' or 'student success coaches'" (p. 15).

Because of this significant overlap of roles and responsibilities across coaches, advisers, and mentors, C-BEN chose to combine the terms to *coaching/advising/mentoring* in its exploratory research (Cleary et al., 2015). For purposes of this document, we will use the term *coach*, though we acknowledge that institutions may use various terms for these functions. See Figure 5.4 for the roles and responsibilities commonly found in the role of a coach.

The role of the coach is robust, and for many institutions the coach is the constant throughout the learners' program, staying with students from admissions (if not preadmissions) through completion. At Westminster College, Seifert and Chapman (2015) shifted from being professors to coaches, providing a keen insight into the two roles. They cited the benefits of being a coach in a competency-based program as (a) building stronger relationships with students; (b) enhancing student performance, including noncontent-related performance; and (c) better representing the kind of relationship that students have outside of the university. However, they also cited the challenges of the coaching role as needing proper training, providing careful and thoughtful scheduling with learners, and setting clear boundaries.

As a CBE leader, you need to have clear roles and responsibilities and an institution-wide understanding of faculty and coaches. But how do faculty and coaches work together in serving learners in

Figure 5.4. Coach responsibilities.

Coaching Activities

1. Explain the CBE program: How does it differ from a traditional approach? What will the student experience be like?
2. Track student progress (typically through use of technology such as dashboards).
3. Motivate students to progress.
4. Refer students to appropriate support services (i.e., writing centers, math assistance).
5. Assist students in setting goals and means for achieving those goals.
6. Guide students on the sequence of competencies for program completion.
7. Assist students in navigating dashboards and other technology-based tools.
8. Inform and assist students with institutional policies and procedures.
9. Collaborate with faculty and staff in meeting student needs.
10. Proactively check in with students.
11. Identify at-risk students and refer them to appropriate services and/or staff.
12. Assist with navigation of systems and regulations such as financial aid and attendance.
13. Assist students in following degree plans.
14. Keep up-to-date records of student progress and needs.

a CBE program? To see one model of the roles and responsibilities of faculty and coaches, let's review another institutional case study.

Brandman University offers two direct assessment competency-based undergraduate programs: Bachelor of Business Administration and Bachelor of Science in Information Technology. Brandman University has two faculty models; the first model is for its traditional credit-based programs in which full-time faculty teach in online and blended courses. The credit-hour full-time faculty teach, develop courses, write and grade assessments, and conduct internal (i.e., university committees) and external (i.e., discipline-related community work) service and mentoring. The second faculty model is for the competency-based programs, and the full-time tutorial faculty are primarily responsible for ensuring that students understand concepts and content, working with students individually. At Brandman University, tutorial faculty are qualified in their discipline and are responsible for discipline-related competencies. For example, the accounting tutorial faculty serve the competencies with accounting content, and the English tutorial faculty serve the competencies with writing and literature as their main focus. In this way, learners have subject matter experts on board to assist with the academic content. Brandman University's students in the CBE programs are served by three separate faculty roles plus an academic coach (Olson & Klein-Collins, 2015).

1. *Curriculum developers.* The faculty who are subject matter experts designed the competency-based modules, including the competencies, learning objectives, curriculum and learning activities, and formative and summative assessments. These faculty members were primarily full-time.

2. *Tutorial faculty.* The tutorial faculty are subject matter experts whose primary responsibility is to instruct learners enrolled in the competency-based program. The tutorial faculty instruct learners in the competencies that are relevant to their discipline. Tutorial faculty ensure that concepts are understood and questions are answered and provide individual and customized instruction for those in need.

3. *Assessment graders.* The assessment graders are subject matter experts whose focus is to use rubrics to accurately and reliably score student submissions of performance-based summative assessment. Assessment graders are currently full-time tutorial faculty, but as the program goes to scale, they will be trained adjunct faculty. Assessment graders provide robust feedback to students for each submission.

4. *Academic coaches.* The academic coaches are the advisers who counsel students regarding their degree requirements and academic policies, encourage and motivate students' progress and engagement, answer questions and refer students to appropriate student support offices and tutorial faculty as needed, and are the go-to person throughout the students' program.

Student Support and Services Staff

In addition to faculty and coaches, there are many other roles and responsibilities of staff that provide student support and services, ensuring success for learners in competency-based programs. Much like in traditional credit-hour programs, the life cycle of learners in CBE programs begins in recruitment and preadmissions and goes through graduation. Staff serving learners in CBE programs need additional development and expertise in CBE to best serve learners in competency-based programs.

The many ways that institutions address the student support and service needs of learners in competency-based programs range from expanding the roles and responsibilities of existing staff with CBE-related development and training to hiring new staff with expertise in competency-based programs. Needless to say, there is no one right answer, and institutions will need to determine the best approach for supporting learners, keeping in mind budget implications.

As a first step, CBE leaders may wish to map out the learners' life cycle at the institution from recruitment to graduation. Once this mapping has occurred, leaders might find it helpful to address the following questions for each key area:

1. Will the existing functions of this office adequately serve learners in competency-based programs?
2. If existing functions are adequate, what additional professional development or training is needed?
3. If existing functions are not adequate, what additional resources or staff are needed to best meet the needs of learners in competency-based programs?

These key questions will need to be explored for all major units, departments, and offices that serve learners. CBE leaders may wish to create a task force to talk through each office, service, and staff and develop a recommended plan of action. This deep dive will also help inform the development of the CBE business model and budget.

The following list includes some offices, units, and staff to consider regarding their roles and responsibilities in serving learners in CBE programs:

- Marketing
- Recruitment
- Enrollment coaching
- Admissions
- Business office
- Financial aid
- Writing and math centers
- Tutorial centers
- Outreach
- Partnerships with employers
- Disability and accommodation office
- Registrar
- Institutional research
- Information technology
- Human resources
- Training and development
- Center for teaching and learning

CBE leaders may find it helpful to review the offices and key staff that CBE learners may engage in throughout their time at the institution. A priority list of key functions may help to establish a work plan for CBE-related development and training, as well as key hires needed.

Considerations for Building Faculty and Staff Models

Although CBE programs have been offered at some institutions for many years, this new emerging model of CBE requires an intentional and transparent approach to curricular design with clearly outlined competencies that must be mastered by students. The use of technology is an integral part of the curriculum and learners' educational journey, as well as in assessment. The role of faculty is evolving, and there are additional or retrained support staff such as coaches needed to ensure student success. All of these elements influence how an institution builds its faculty and staff models.

Desrochers and Staisloff (2016) studied the business models and costs of four institutions offering CBE programs. There are three major elements across these institutions that have the potential to significantly affect faculty and staff models and their subsequent cost and business models. These major elements include the following:

1. *A different approach to curriculum development and delivery.* This includes the process for designing a CBE program from competencies to assessments to learning activities. Considerations include delivery method (online or on-ground or combination) and textbooks and/or open education resources.

2. *A new faculty model.* This encompasses the unbundled and reassembled faculty model for areas such as curriculum development, program creation, assessment, instruction, and grading. There is also consideration of student-to-faculty ratios: What is best to meet learners' needs?

3. *A new student experience.* This focuses on the creation of an integrated, cross-disciplinary approach to reduce redundancies in programs, which leads to increased efficiency and less time to degree. Students can advance through the programs at flexible rates.

The building of faculty and staff models for CBE programs is the strategic foundation for an institution to determine what is needed to ensure student success. CBE leaders with their CBE team can benefit from learning what other CBE institutions needed to create the best fit for their institution and their students. It is important to keep in mind that these models may need to be altered as we learn what works and what continues to be a challenge, and they may need revision.

Conclusion

CBE leaders will need to build an institution-wide team of faculty and staff to build, implement, and sustain a successful CBE program. Looking inside at existing roles and responsibilities of staff and faculty is a good first step. Looking outside to other institutions that offer CBE programs will help immensely in building faculty and staff models. Adopt and adapt liberally the information provided in the tables to determine what is needed and who will fulfill that role. On the basis of institutional culture, learners' needs, and current faculty and staff models, build the program that will be the best fit while allowing for flexibility for change as we learn what is working and what is not.

6

BUSINESS MODELS, PROCESSES, AND SYSTEMS

A competency-based education (CBE) program clearly affects the entire institution in fundamental ways. Changes to the faculty and staff roles have been discussed along with deep shifts in curriculum design and delivery. However, the breadth of change required to successfully implement and scale a CBE program might not be so obvious to the institutional leader considering this option. There is an old saying regarding the assumption of "normal" in any given situation: "Does a fish know it's in water? Not until it is removed." In higher education, our "normal" (or "water" in this metaphor) is the credit hour—most of our processes, systems, and business models are rooted in this metric of the credit hour. Nearly all of higher education's back office processes use credit-hour assumptions in one way or the other. Everything from tuition models to faculty pay models is commonly based on this shared metric. Our technology is built around this assumption, and our worldview is deeply rooted in this "standardized" measure. The impact to the institution is much larger than the learning delivery model, and it is essential that fully informed decisions are made at each step of program design, implementation, and efforts to scale.

This chapter will introduce the challenges and potential solutions to some of these issues, including those with technology (the *learning management system* [LMS] and the *student information system* [SIS]), financial aid delivery models, financial aid software, student billing, and emerging business models for CBE programs.

One important lesson from leaders who have guided the development and implementation of CBE programs is that the managers of these areas must be brought into the design and development of this program early in the process. However, these managers must be expected to arrive with an innovation and solution-oriented mind-set. Many of these managers have worked hard to develop and scale systems and processes that are at once compliant with regulations and efficient. They are often understandably protective of these models, and institutional leaders must be clear in their expectations that solutions will be found for the CBE challenges.

Technology

As mentioned in chapter 1, technology is one of the areas most affected by a CBE program. Many of these systems can feel "invisible" until we need them to be different. In fact, in 2015, 79% of Competency-Based Education Network institutions stated that inadequate technology for CBE presented significant barriers to operation (Leuba, 2015). As a result of this finding, the Technical Interoperability Pilot project was initiated. In this project, five important institutional needs were identified, and vendors participated in generating pilot solutions for those issues. This is an important project for the following key reasons: (a) It focused on interoperability for the technology systems, and (b) it countered the common objection by providers that CBE was just too variable for them to develop meaningful responses (Leuba, 2015). The five projects identified for this are as follows:

1. *Managing competencies rather than courses.* The challenge here is the issue of registering students for units of competencies rather than courses. This requires a method of unique identification for competencies and a way to track students' progress toward credential completion.
2. *Capturing competency ratings rather than grades.* From the LMS to the SIS, grades are expected to be entered, and the grade options are generally A, B, C, D, F, and P/F. If competency levels are to be tracked, a different option is required,

and this information must be passed from any grade book in the LMS to the SIS for official record keeping.

3. *Providing program information for nonterm financial aid delivery.* Nonterm financial aid can offer students the most flexibility in their journey to a credential; however, it is also very complex to administer. Most SIS and financial aid software is not capable of supporting this process.

4. *Measuring faculty–student interaction.* One requirement for high-quality CBE programs is that there is interaction between faculty and students. As of 2017, this is also a regulatory requirement for federal financial aid to be delivered to students in these programs. To both monitor and provide evidence of this interaction, the LMS has to be able to track and document these interactions.

5. *Providing extended transcripts.* New models of transcripts are emerging, and this is more fully discussed in the following section. Ideally, transcripts of credentials earned in CBE programs have two components: (a) documentation of the competency demonstrated and credential earned, and (b) a "crosswalk" back to a credit-bearing model for these competencies and credentials. Although many might think that a more "pure" CBE model might not make this translation back to credit hours, it is important for the student. For students to successfully transfer, apply to graduate schools, or qualify for employer reimbursement, they often need documentation of credits earned and even grades. This is an important service for students, who ought to be "held harmless" as CBE programs integrate effectively with traditional higher education, but this can be a significant technology challenge. (Leuba, 2015)

Learning Management System

Whether the academic program will be delivered face-to-face, online, or in a hybrid model, the LMS can play an essential role. Considerations when selecting an LMS for the CBE program can be clustered into the following groups: (a) alignment to academic vision, (b) alignment to institutional resources, (c) integration with other systems on campus, and (d) data and student support capabilities and integrations. Each of these will be considered separately, although there is significant overlap across them.

Alignment to academic vision. The CBE program must have an academic vision, and the LMS must be selected to align with and support this vision. For example, if the program envisions peer group activities as an essential component of the program, the LMS ought to be able to support and even enable this sort of work. The LMS has many different capabilities, so it is important that the CBE team has articulated its top academic design priorities. Even very basic questions must be asked. Consider what happens when the CBE design team wants to offer only "competent" or "not competent" as evaluative ratings for the competency demonstrations, but the LMS offers only "pass" or "fail." Is that good enough for the CBE program? Why or why not? Other considerations might include capability for video presentations by students (to provide increased authenticity in the assessments), ability to display progress toward credential or competency completion, calendaring functions that might serve to keep students on track, automated reminders, grade book capabilities to capture competencies, and ability to track faculty–student interaction.

Alignment to institutional resources. The LMS must be supported by the staff in the institution, and different LMSs require different skill sets and different resources.

Integration with other systems on campus. As discussed previously, the LMS is a critical capability for the CBE program. But the LMS is only one part of the larger technology ecosystem supporting the university in general and the CBE program specifically. When leaders are selecting the LMS, it is important to ensure that it is easily integrated with the other technology being used on the campus. Although it is usually possible to integrate systems, some integrations can be more challenging than others. It can be useful to ask the LMS provider about experience with integrations at other institutions.

Data and student support capabilities and integrations. It is also important that the LMS supports data collection and reporting. When selecting the LMS, leaders should inquire about data analytics and reporting capabilities. Some LMSs have built analytics and proactive reports regarding student progress and engagement into the faculty or administrative dashboards, whereas others depend on institutions to do these analyses themselves. In the latter case, it is important that the platform supports data exporting.

Student Information System

The SIS often serves as a backbone for the institution. It is essential that the SIS be able to support (at least minimally) the CBE program. As mentioned in the previous discussion on the Technical Interoperability Pilot project, it can be challenging for SISs to track competency attainment rather than course completion. Even this simple-sounding difference can cause tremendous manual work and frustration for staff and students. The SIS is a foundation for the transcript in many cases, so this integration is essential. The SIS has to support the academic vision, including the vision for the transcript (or comprehensive student record), as discussed next. It is important to recognize that institutions will (for the most part) not choose to operate two separate SISs, so the challenge becomes a configuration solution for the SIS, which meets more traditional needs but can be adapted to meet the needs of a CBE program as well.

Transcript and Comprehensive Student Record

A tremendous amount of work has been done regarding the transcription of competencies. Both individual institutions and collaborations between professional organizations are helping to move this effort forward. One example is the Comprehensive Student Record project, a partnership between the American Association of Collegiate Registrars and Admissions Officers (AACRAO) and NASPA: Student Affairs Administrators in Higher Education to advance different methods of tracking students' academic progress. Goals of this project include to "directly assist a group of twelve institutions to develop models of comprehensive student records that may include: 1. Competency-based education; 2. Learning outcomes for programs/majors/degrees; and/or 3. Co-curricular learning records and outcomes" (Strausheim, 2016). Among these 12 institutions, some have created prototypes such as the one shown in Figure 6.1 to move this work forward.

A more radically disruptive part of the movement to create a next-gen transcript is the Credential Registry. This registry describes itself as a new approach to capturing, connecting, archiving, and sharing information about credentials (among other things), including degrees, certificates, certifications, licenses, apprenticeships, badges, microcredentials, and more (Credential Registry, 2017). Although this specific project might not be critical for every CBE program, it will be important for leaders of CBE programs to remain aware of this sort of disaggregation of the degree and credential into competencies and microcredentials.

On a more fundamental level, it will be important for institutions to work with their transcript provider (whether these are generated internally from SIS-based information or generated by an external vendor) to design a transcript that both aligns with the academic vision of the CBE program and complies with external expectations. Knowledge of efforts such as those mentioned earlier can be very helpful in offering options and alleviating worries to registrars and others in academic affairs who might be concerned about transcript changes.

Figure 6.1. Extended transcript prototype example (IMS Global).

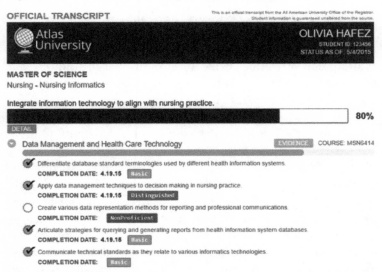

Note. From "An Evolving Technology Landscape for Competency-Based Education," by M. Leuba, 2016, February 22, EDUCAUSE Review. Retrieved from http://er.educause.edu/articles/2016/2/an-evolving-technology-landscape-for-competency-based-education

Financial Aid

One way to describe the range of current CBE programs is to place programs along the continuum shown in Figure 6.2. As leaders make decisions regarding where along this continuum their CBE program will operate, they have to consider the implications across the institution. Financial aid is one area for which this decision has significant implications. If the goal is to maximize student flexibility and speed to credential, the direct assessment model offers the richest possibility. It also has the most complex and unclear approval pathway, it has the largest set of challenges from an infrastructure perspective, and there are still regulatory limitations on flexibility. (There is more on regulatory issues in chapter 7.)

If the direct assessment model is chosen, financial aid delivery becomes significantly more complex. Financial aid for direct assessment in the nonterm environment is difficult to explain to students and challenging to operationalize. However, when the direct assessment model is offered on a nonterm basis, students can move continuously through to their credential without predetermined breaks or ends of term. Other financial aid regulations still apply and can limit student's flexibility, but overall students are much more "in charge" of their pacing in this model. Limits include things such as satisfactory academic progress policies, regular and substantive engagement expectations, and academic calendar definitions. In the direct assessment model,

Figure 6.2. CBE framework continuum.

Course-based, term-based, credit-hour-based competencies defined in single courses	No courses, no terms, no credit hours Competencies defined at credential level

Learning measured by seat time (credits) and assessed by classroom instructor	Learning measured by direct assessment of competency with authentic, transparent, and aligned assessment

people often like to say that students can move "as quickly as they are able or as slowly as is needed" to demonstrate competency. In reality, there is a minimal speed limit based on the satisfactory academic progress expectations. This is not necessarily bad, because no one wants students to borrow or pay money without making good progress toward a credential. This is another good example of the need for the academic vision to be well integrated with the realities of current regulations and expectations.

If a leader determines it is most important to reduce the disruption to the systems on campus, the leader can choose to operate the CBE program further to the left on the continuum. CBE programs can be delivered well in a term-based, credit-bearing model. One just has to understand the limitations inherent in that choice. Limitations include the need for students to have completed competencies by the end of a standard term, rather than at "their own pace," and the need to comply with expectations regarding seat time for the credits being earned and expectations for weekly academic engagement. In this model, there is very little change to financial aid delivery from the traditional term-based model. The U.S. Department of Education has offered guidance regarding CBE in a few Dear Colleague letters and other resources (U.S. Department of Education, 2013, 2014). The most recently released resource answers questions about participating in the U.S. Department of Education's experimental sites and is a good overall resource to learn more about how this group views CBE and disbursing federal financial aid. This guide is called the *Competency-Based Education Reference Guide* (U.S. Department of Education, Federal Student Aid, 2016).

A leader should also consider the impact of any decisions on active military students or veterans. Some institutions have reached agreements with their regional VA benefits teams to allow vets to attend direct assessment programs, but the Department of Defense has not been eager to embrace this approach and support it through tuition assistance.

Business Models

One of the most commonly mentioned potential benefits of CBE is the hope that these programs can be a lower cost to institutions and thus to students. The student cost savings is achieved in two primary ways: lowered tuition and speed to credential. Among those students for whom flexibility is a priority over speed, there might not be significant tuition savings. And, of course, for institutions, the potentially shorter time a successful CBE student will spend paying tuition puts pressure on the traditional revenue model. This can be partially offset by increased retention rates of new students, and early results support the assumption that CBE programs can deliver higher retention rates (Desrochers & Staisloff, 2016; Parsons, Mason, & Soldner, 2016).

The business model is necessarily interdependent with the academic model and the financial aid approach selected. One central component in any institution of higher education's business model is its set of tuition and pricing assumptions. Interestingly, most programs choosing a direct assessment academic model have also chosen a subscription model for tuition. The subscription model has a couple of key advantages for both the institution and the student: It incentivizes the student to persist and make good progress within each payment period, and it avoids potential over-borrowing that could occur if a student were moving quickly and tuition were still credit bound.

Desrochers and Staisloff (2016) reviewed the business models for four emerging CBE players and were able to identify key strategic questions leaders should ask themselves as they enter into the CBE arena. Each of these questions reflect decision points that influence the level of up-front investment required to launch a CBE program. The questions are as follows, each with a short explanation of its significance in the CBE program's business model development:

1. Will the institution create a model that holds learning constant and allows time to vary (such as through Direct Assessment)? Or, will the institution take a credit-bearing course model and map program-level learning outcomes and competencies to it? (Desrochers and Staisloff, 2016, p. 32)

    As mentioned previously, this is a pivotal decision that drives many additional decisions and investments. If the institution decided on a direct assessment model, there is likely much greater financial demand in the early years. In fact, Desrochers and Staisloff (2016) found that during the first year of instruction, spending on the CBE program averaged

$4.1 million, or $52,500 per student enrolled. Total expenditures ranged from about $800,000 to $5.8 million, while per-student spending ranged from less than $20,000 to more than $100,000 per student. These average expenditures per student reflect that low initial enrollment, and these metrics are expected to decline significantly as enrollment increases.

2. How will the institution balance price, efficiency, and scale questions in setting expectations and moving toward a sustainable business model? How will making low price the primary driver of the business model affect other key levers, such as the unbundling of traditional roles and the numbers of students who will need to be educated for the program to break even? (Desrochers and Staisloff, 2016, p. 32)

   For some institutions, a low tuition price was a primary driver behind this innovation. In this case, institutions committed to a price prior to knowing much about how students in these programs would actually behave. This commitment not only limited the flexibility of the business model but also drove designers to build programs with price in mind. This is a truly unusual exercise for much of higher education, where tuition is simply raised to meet the need of the institution's budget.

3. How will the CBE design initiative support a reevaluation of learning activities and faculty roles to produce high-quality learning and student success? (Desrochers and Staisloff, 2016, p. 32)

   Strong outcomes will be essential to the scalability of these CBE programs, and a continuous improvement mindset will be needed to ensure high-quality learning. Although this will potentially add some cost to the equation for institutions, it needs to be viewed as a key part of the overall investment in the program.

4. What is the institution's ability to invest in new technology to support learning management and student information? Given the rapid changes in technology, how will the institution keep this technology current? (Desrochers and Staisloff, 2016, p. 32)

   As discussed previously, new technologies are required to bring these models to scale, particularly when the academic model lands on the more disruptive side of the continuum.

5. How long is the institution willing and able to support a new CBE program until breakeven is achieved, and at what cost? (Desrochers and Staisloff, 2016, p. 32)

   Desrochers and Staisloff (2016) reported that institutions expect their CBE programs to begin to be profitable between five and six years post launch. Leaders must understand this reality, and their governing boards must also support this longer term investment (see Figure 6.3).

6. What opportunities exist for federal, state, and local governments to promote and fund shared services that would support multiple institutions at reduced costs? (Desrochers and Staisloff, 2016, p. 32)

   One way to bring CBE programs to market more quickly would be to gain the support of possible funders. In fact, there is a need for most state-funding formulae to change if they are to effectively support CBE, because most state formulae are also rooted in credit-hour production by the institution.

Although initial development costs are higher in academic, technology, and marketing areas during program development and initial launch, Desrochers and Staisloff (2016) reported that institutions expect these expenses to decline significantly once these programs are built and established. In addition, it is clear that building new, nonterm-based CBE programs from the ground up requires higher levels of investment than creating CBE programs that more closely adhere to traditional academic terms and the credit hour.

Figure 6.3. Average CBE expenditure per student, four institutions.

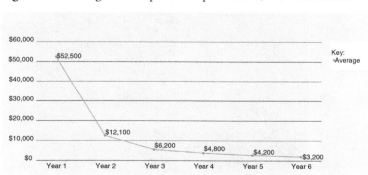

It is useful to note that these business model decisions also have a ripple effect across the institution. For example, in a direct assessment, nonterm model, faculty members' work is very different. They have students at all variety of stages of their program, and there are no set term breaks for faculty to take time away. Many faculty-pay models rely on credits as a backbone to workload allocation, and without a credit equivalency, it can be challenging to determine a fair workload and pay model for faculty. All of this affects the cost of the program to the institution and ultimately to the student.

Conclusion

Offering a CBE program can affect every process and assumption across institutional departments. It is important for the leader considering a CBE program to be prepared for this and to support early engagement across departments with a solution mind-set. It is also important for leaders to understand that CBE programs are an investment in advancing our higher education model. This investment pays off in instructional reputation and preparedness for the future rather than in short-term net revenue gains. CBE program leaders must monitor investments and business model assumptions carefully but must also travel a patient path with an eye toward the larger goal.

7

APPROVAL
CONSIDERATIONS

Once an institution has made the complex set of decisions outlined in the previous chapters regarding its emerging competency-based education (CBE) program, it is essential for leadership to articulate the pathway to launch. Approvals—both internal and external—are important milestones on this pathway to a program launch. Ideally, leaders developing the CBE program have already taken the time to understand both the processes and the regulatory requirements to achieve internal and external approvals for this new program. In fact, an understanding of these requirements can be effectively used to influence design decisions. For example, if the institution does not want to expend the time and energy required for direct assessment approvals, it would be important to create a program that aligned with the accreditation and regulatory expectations for a term-based, credit-hour-bearing CBE program. It can be exceedingly frustrating and demoralizing to a team working hard on the design of a new CBE program to learn at the end of the process about limitations or approval requirements for which they are unprepared. The continuum presented in chapter 6 can also be useful at this point (see Figure 6.2).

In addition to the CBE continuum, an institution will have to consider issues such as delivery modality, current institutional degree and program-level approvals, and external requirements for the credential being earned.

As previously discussed, CBE programs can be offered in a traditional face-to-face modality, in a distance education format, or in a blended or hybrid format. If the CBE program is designed to be delivered via distance education, the institution will need to be sure that it either already has the approvals needed for distance education from its accreditor or is prepared to acquire that approval. In addition, leaders will need to consider the issue of state authorizations for this distance education offering. If the CBE program is to be offered outside of the institution's home state, leaders will need to familiarize themselves with the process of state authorization and potentially with NC-SARA (National Council for State Authorization Reciprocity Agreements, http:// nc-sara.org).

Another variable that can add complexity to the approval processes is the types of degrees and programs for which the institution is currently approved. For example, if leaders believe that an MBA degree would be a good place to start for the institution in building CBE programs, but the institution does not have approval for graduate degrees and has no undergraduate business program, this would raise red flags for some approvals. Ideally, the institution would already be approved for the degree level (associate's, bachelor's, master's, doctoral) and the content area (e.g., business, nursing, IT) in which the CBE program would be offered. It is certainly not impossible to start the CBE program in a new institutional space, but it will involve more approvals.

Yet another consideration involves the credential being offered and its external stakeholders. For example, do graduates from this program need to be licensed in order to practice or work? If so, then the CBE program must align to the requirements for licensure. This can be challenging, because many licensure requirements still talk about hours needed rather than learning outcomes. Some licensing bodies have been willing to work this through with CBE programs, but others have not. This will also vary state to state and thus can require of the organization significant amounts of information to support students toward reaching their goals. Specialized accreditation (or programmatic accreditation) can also be required by some licensing boards. It will be important to understand if there is a relevant (and necessary) programmatic accreditor for the proposed CBE program. If the answer is yes, leaders should connect with that accreditor as soon as possible to understand the requirements and garner support for the CBE program.

Approvals Pathway

The pathway to both internal and external approvals can be bumpy, but it is smoothed by efforts to generate buy-in from those involved in the approval processes. Innovations such as CBE programming can cause alarm, skepticism, or simple resistance in many people, including those who are assigned (either formally or informally) to monitor quality in higher education. As CBE continues on its growth trajectory, many misunderstandings and biases are also emerging. Clear, direct information about how the institution's CBE program will actually operate will be useful in correcting misunderstandings and assuaging anxieties. For example, some people may believe that CBE programs will cause faculty or staff to lose their jobs. This sort of underlying misinformation must be corrected before constituents will be able to effectively consider the real pros and cons of a CBE program.

There is substantial literature on managing change and improvement within organizations (Kotter, 2012, 2014). Nearly all of them agree that preparing and planning for the change is of equal importance to identifying the need for change or implementing the change. Change management approaches emphasize the need for a clear rationale for the change and opportunity to discuss and gather input on components of the change by the affected employees. These methods can be very useful for leaders to gain buy-in for the CBE program, thus increasing the likelihood of gaining the necessary approvals. This planning is important for both internal approvals and external approvals.

Table 7.1 is not intended to be exhaustive, but it serves as a possible framework for the approval process for a new CBE program. Because each institution's shared governance process is slightly different, the fifth column is intended to serve as a worksheet in which a leader can identify which of these potential approvals is relevant for the CBE program being launched at the leader's institution. The first column identifies the type of approval that might be needed. The second and third columns are

TABLE 7.1
Possible Framework for the Approval Process for a New CBE Program

Approval Type	For Direct Assessment	For CBE	New to Distance Education?	New Degree or Discipline	Your Institution
Departmental approval	R	R	R	R	
College-level curriculum committee approval	R	R	R	R	
Dean approval	R	R	R	R	
University-level curriculum committee approval	R	Depends	R	R	
Provost approval	R	R	R	R	
Academic council or cabinet approvals?	R	Depends	R	R	
Senior leadership team approvals	R	R	R	R	
President approval	R	R	R	R	
University academic affairs committee or board approval	R	Depends	Depends	R	
University board approval	R	Depends	Depends	R	
System approval	If appropriate	If appropriate	If appropriate	If appropriate	
State-level approval	R	Depends	R	R	
Institutional accreditor approval	R	Depends	R	R	
Specialized accreditor approval	Depends	Depends	Depends	Depends	
U.S. Department of Education approval (required for federal financial aid)	R	Depends	Depends	R	

Note. R = a most likely required gate in the approval pathway.

intended to differentiate the requirements for a direct assessment program versus a CBE program. The fourth and fifth columns summarize the issue discussed earlier regarding new degree program levels or delivery modality. The "R" in the columns indicates that this is most likely a required gate in the approval pathway.

As one can see from Table 7.1, the pathway to approval (even internal to the institution) is lengthy. For innovations such as CBE, issues such as quality and reputational concerns will be raised throughout the approval process. It is essential not only that the internal approval processes are followed and accepted but also that there is a clear and consistent signal that the institution's leadership is conceptually on board.

Critical Decisions

Because the approval pathway varies dependent on the design of the CBE programs to be launched, it can be helpful to make some critical decisions as early as possible in the design cycle. Clarity about the vision for the program will expedite both internal and external approval processes. Some of the most pivotal decisions are to

- retain the credit hour or apply for direct assessment;
- retain the term-based model or move to a nonterm financial aid model;
- deliver face-to-face education, distance education, or a hybrid;
- role of faculty and staff is to retain current structures or change them; and
- gain approvals for federal financial aid for students in the CBE program or not.

Once the basic architecture for the program has been decided, it is important to bring your internal experts into the planning discussions. Innovation always involves creating solutions within limitations, and it will be important to design your CBE program with regulatory compliance in mind. This can be particularly important if you want to allow your students access to federal financial aid. If federal financial aid will be important to your students, your financial aid experts need to be in the design conversations from the beginning. Gathering insight from these internal experts will ensure that your CBE program has important features (e.g., regular and substantive interaction with faculty) and important capabilities (e.g., the ability to track student interaction with faculty). In addition, failure to engage key players such as the financial aid team can generate significant internal resistance to needed program approvals.

As the CBE program moves through the various gates needed to gain full approval, it is very likely that changes and adaptations will be needed as external approvers express feedback or concerns about particular features or processes in the program. Unfortunately, it is also likely that different approvers will offer conflicting advice or input. It will also be important for leaders to remain aware of shifting external expectations and circumstances related to CBE. As mentioned previously, there have been investigations from the inspector general at the U.S. Department of Education that have caused changes in expectations from accreditors and other regulators (Fain, 2015a, 2016).

In these cases, it will be important that the institution be able to explain the rationale behind its decisions and choices. Many times, external reviewers will have some flexibility as long as the institution's rationale is strong and clear.

Important External Approvals

As discussed previously, the accreditors and regulators involved in approving each CBE program will vary based on a number of things, including the institution's accreditor, the need for a specialized accreditor, the requirements of the institution's home state, the delivery modality, and the design decisions. It is important for leaders to understand the requirements to gain approval from the relevant players.

Regional accreditors. The regional accreditors have differing experience with, processes for, and definitions of *CBE*. Most of the regional accreditors have specific information on their websites to guide institutions through the CBE (or direct assessment) approval processes. All of the regional accreditors cite the work of the Council of Regional Accrediting Commissions (2015) to create a shared framework for and definition of *CBE* and the accrediting process (see Table 7.2).

TABLE 7.2
Regional Accreditors

Higher Learning Commission	www.hlcommission.org/Monitoring/competency-based-education-programs.html
WASC Senior College and University Commission	www.wscuc.org/content/substantive-change-manual
WASC (ACCJC)	wascarc.org/sites/default/files/_Binder_Subchange.pdf
New England Association of Schools and Colleges	cihe.neasc.org/institutional-reports-resources/reporting-guidelines/substantive-change-proposals
Southern Association of Colleges and Schools Commission on Colleges	www.sacscoc.org/pdf/081705/DirectAssessmentCompetencyBased.pdf
Middle States Commission on Higher Education	www.msche.org/documents/CBEScreeningFormOctober2015.pdf
Northwest Commission on Colleges and Universities	www.nwccu.org/Standards%20and%20Policies/Policies/PolicyDocs/Substantive%20Change%20Policy%20-%202017.pdf

National accreditors. The national accreditors do not all address CBE directly. However, the Distance Education Accrediting Commission (DEAC) has successfully accredited CBE programs, enabling at least one program to participate in the U.S. Department of Education's CBE experimental sites. The landscape is changing rapidly, and leaders at nationally accredited institutions will need to connect with their accreditor to understand both the requirements and the processes for approval of any CBE program.

Programmatic or specialized accreditors. Programmatic accreditors are increasingly able to incorporate the structure and processes of CBE programs into the requirements for their accreditation. Notably, the Commission on Collegiate Nursing Education (CCNE) has retained programmatic accreditation in at least two CBE-based nursing programs. More programmatic accreditors are exploring their options and following the CCNE's lead.

U.S. Department of Education. If the institutional leaders decide that access to federal financial aid is important for their students, there are several design considerations that must be taken seriously. Some of these requirements and relevant citations for further information are highlighted as follows:

1. *Faculty-initiated regular and substantive interaction.* This is a design requirement for CBE programs. The terms are defined as follows: *Regular* means the interaction cannot be optional and cannot be solely at the initiation of the student; *substantive* can include direct instruction, substantive feedback to assessments, or contacts with students that create the opportunity for relevant discussion of academic subject matter; and *instructor* means the interaction is provided by institutional staff who meet accrediting agency standards for providing instruction in the subject matter being discussed. In addition, the following two conditions must be met: The interaction must be faculty initiated, and the students must have ready access to faculty. If automated solutions or staff not qualified as faculty are initiating the contact, students must have ready access to faculty.

2. *Satisfactory academic progress.* New methods of tracking progress and calculating satisfactory academic progress will be needed in a CBE program. Volume 3 of the *Federal Student Aid Handbook* (U.S. Department of Education, 2017) describes the requirements for an institution's Satisfactory Academic Progress (SAP) policy. The experimental sites reference guide also offers examples of how SAP might be managed in a variety of CBE programs (U.S. Department of Education, 2016).

3. *Academic engagement and educational activity.* For all CBE programs, including direct assessment programs, educational activity includes, but is not limited to, the following:
   - Participating in regularly scheduled learning sessions (where there is an opportunity for direct interaction between the student and the faculty member)
   - Submitting an academic assignment
   - Taking an exam, an interactive tutorial, or computer-assisted instruction

- Attending a study group that is assigned by the institution
- Participating in an online discussion about academic matters
- Consulting with a faculty mentor to discuss academic course content
- Participating in faculty-guided independent study (as defined in 34 CFR 668.10[a][3][iii])

For direct assessment programs only, educational activity also includes development of an academic action plan developed in consultation with a qualified faculty member that addresses competencies identified by the institution (U.S. Department of Education, Federal Student Aid, 2016).

4. *Blending of credit bearing and direct assessment.* This is not allowed. Unless the institution is participating in the CBE experimental site for CBE, a student cannot be enrolled in a program that is a hybrid of direct assessment and credit bearing. In the language of the Dear Colleague letter of 2014,

> Unlike CBE programs offered in credit or clock hours, there is a specific federal definition for direct assessment programs. A direct assessment program is an instructional program that, in lieu of credit hours or clock hours as measures of student learning, utilizes direct assessment of student learning, or recognizes the direct assessment of student learning by others. The assessment must be consistent with the accreditation of the institution or program utilizing the results of the assessment. Direct assessment of student learning means a measure by the institution of what a student knows and can do in terms of the body of knowledge making up the educational program. These measures provide evidence that a student has mastered a specific subject, content area, or skill or that the student demonstrates a specific quality such as creativity, analysis or synthesis associated with the subject matter of the program. Examples of direct measures include projects, papers, examinations, presentations, performances, and portfolios. Student progress is measured solely using direct assessment. Therefore, unlike a CBE program measured in credit or clock hours, a direct assessment program does not specify the level of educational activity in which a student is

expected to engage in order to complete the program. However, because a direct assessment program does not utilize credit or clock hours as a measure of student learning, an institution must establish a methodology to reasonably equate the direct assessment program (or the direct assessment portion of any program, as applicable) to credit or clock hours for the purpose of complying with applicable regulatory requirements. Note that even though student progress in a direct assessment program is measured without credit or clock hours, an institution may still provide credit or clock hour equivalents on a student's transcript in order to facilitate the transfer of credit to other institutions. In such a case, institutional policies, publications and consumer information must be clear in specifying that the program is a direct assessment program rather than a clock or credit hour program. Before an institution may provide Title IV aid to students in a direct assessment program, that program must be approved under the regulatory provisions at 34 CFR 668.10. (U.S. Department of Education, 2014)

Other Considerations and Cautions

There are several other cautions that will be important for leaders to understand.

Prior learning assessment (PLA). Although PLA is rooted in a competency approach to learning, it is distinct from a CBE program. It is important to remember that federal financial aid does not include PLA in the student's aid package. This is primarily rooted in the belief that financial aid is "paying for" teaching rather than validation of learning. Although this position might be interesting to debate, it is the current guideline. It will be important to specify if and when PLA will be assessed and granted by the institution, and it must be separated from matriculation in the CBE program.

"Crosswalk" to credit hours. When CBE programs are developed, they must demonstrate how they are related to credit hours. For direct assessment applications, this is an important topic to navigate both internally and when applying for approvals. If the program is completely linked to credit hours, it will likely be deemed to be a CBE program that is credit bearing. Either way,

it will be essential that the translation from competency to credit-hour equivalency is clear, transparent, and consistently communicated to internal constituents, students, and external bodies.

Apprenticeships or clinical requirements. Most often, clinical requirements and apprenticeships have requirements about the number of hours spent in the activity. This can pose a challenge to CBE programs, but it is important to remember that the students' needs have the highest priority. If an external licensing or credentialing body requires calculation and reporting of hours, it will be important to comply. As a community, CBE leaders ought to be challenging these requirements, but as long as they stand, the students' need for reporting of hours must be met. Of course, institutions can layer competency demonstration requirements "on top of" these time-based requirements, and this adaptation can improve the integrity of the learning experience.

Case Study

Imagine a public four-year institution whose leaders decide that they want to offer a CBE MBA. They already offer a traditional MBA in a face-to-face format. The dean of the business school is convinced that this degree will be a strong offering, and she is able to persuade the provost and president to move ahead with exploring potential costs and benefits. The business school does not hold a specialized accreditation at this time. The dean meets with her chairs and discusses this idea. They are enthusiastic, and the chairs lead the discussions with the faculty of the business school regarding the idea. There is some slight resistance, but the faculty involved with the MBA are open and enthusiastic, partly because they hope that this new program will breathe new life into their college. A small team of faculty begin to work on developing the competencies and program, and in time, the team members develop a proposal for an MBA that is approved for direct assessment and is offered in a distance education format. They gain approval from their department and then from the business school curriculum committee for the degree offering. However, when they present to the University Curriculum Committee (UCC), things do not go well. There is a tremendous amount of misunderstanding regarding CBE on the UCC, and the business faculty are taken by surprise with the level of hostility in the discussion about this new MBA. They decide to regroup, and they develop a plan to educate the larger faculty about CBE, quality, and the role of faculty in the degree offering.

The provost and president learn about this setback and decide that they should begin educating the board about CBE and its fit with the university's mission and goals in order to prevent a similar reaction from the board.

The team in the financial aid office also learns about this faculty discussion and makes an appointment to talk to the dean. The members of the team in financial aid are very concerned about the idea of offering a direct assessment program. They tell the dean about the additional expenses involved with processing financial aid in this way and express concern about the manual processes that might be needed.

The dean realizes that she needs to bring others at the university into this plan as well. She connects with the accreditation liaison and learns that they will need to apply for both direct assessment and distance education approvals. The accreditation liaison advises the dean to also begin to prepare an application for approval for the State Higher Education Office.

The team members reconsider whether the expense and work for direct assessment will make sense for their program, based on this new information. They redesign the MBA to remain credit hour and term based. They prepare applications for approval by the state and their institutional accreditor. Because the MBA will be offered in a distance education format, they decide to affiliate with NC-SARA and prepare that application as well.

These applications are developed while the team is holding important internal conversations and developing a shared university-wide position on CBE. Ultimately, this approach is successful, and the UCC approves the program. Because of the cross-departmental collaboration that developed after the first failed UCC visit, the approval process with the board also goes smoothly.

There are a number of questions from both the state and the accreditor regarding the CBE program, including details such as credit equivalency, transcription, and the role of faculty. The distance education application requires a site visit, so the approvals are a bit more delayed.

The team uses this extra time to fine-tune the curriculum, work on integrating the learning management systems and the student information systems, and streamline any other operational issues that are identified. Ultimately, the state approves the program, and the accreditor approves both the distance education application and the CBE program. The marketing team is poised and ready to release its information. Notification is sent to the institution's liaison at the U.S. Department of Education, who is satisfied that this is not a direct assessment program and thus has no additional requirements.

The leaders are both pleased that the program has been approved and a bit astonished at the process. The dean remarks that she is not entirely sure that she would have ventured forward with this if she had understood the full picture more accurately. However, the university team members are proud of themselves for this innovation and excited to engage with the new students earning an MBA in their CBE program.

8

CONCLUSION AND NEXT STEPS

From a small seed a mighty trunk may grow.

—Aeschylus

If the previous chapters in this book have you thinking about what is possible at your institution, this chapter will provide you with guidance on how to get started. Institutional leaders have great interest in competency-based education (CBE) but often get overwhelmed when they are confronted with the task list of items that must be accomplished to have a program ready for launch. Like with most large projects, when you break tasks down into smaller parts, the work becomes more manageable and less daunting. In the pages that follow, you will discover how to manage the CBE design and implementation process in a more reasonable fashion.

Step 1: Executive Team Creates and Communicates the Overarching Vision

Unless you are the president or the chief academic officer at your institution, you will need to convene your executive leaders so you can share your CBE vision and garner this group's support. Ideally, you are seeking to convene a group composed of the following:

- President or designee
- Chief academic officer or provost

- Chief financial officer
- Institutional leader for strategy, strategic initiatives, or innovation
- Anticipated academic leader (e.g., the dean of the college where the program will be housed)
- Anticipated project champion (which may be you)

You will want to keep this group relatively small and the scope of activity confined to vision casting and the highest level of CBE strategy. Your approach for convening this group depends on your institution, but others have accomplished this in a number of different ways, including writing CBE program proposals, sharing literature on the expansion of CBE, and suggesting a conversation to discuss how your institution should respond. This process could take many weeks to accomplish, especially if you have to work through multiple organizational levels.

Once you have convened this group and garnered its support for the CBE program, it will be responsible for setting the overarching vision for the project. This group should focus on answering questions such as the following:

- How disruptive do you want CBE efforts to be?
- Why would the institution pursue CBE? What's in it for the institution, the faculty and staff, and the students?
- What financial resources can be committed to the effort?
- What are the value propositions for your CBE effort?
- Who is the target audience?
- What type of academic content will be delivered (e.g., business, engineering, information technology)?
- What will the business model be?
- What new or modified technology will be needed?

Many of these types of decisions cannot and should not be made by this group alone. Typically, the earlier others are involved in the decision-making process, the easier it is for others to embrace and adopt a shared vision. Who else needs to be involved varies by institutions, but those with positional authority and those known to influence others would be most helpful.

Part of the executive team's vision casting should be identifying likely barriers, such as information technology, faculty resistance, and the lack of resources. This group should create strategies for getting past these barriers. Sometimes, institutions find the greatest barrier is human resistance. The executive team should give this consideration and identify people who will need to be "sold" on the idea. The team should craft an engagement strategy for bringing these individuals on board and in support of—or, at least, not in active resistance to—the CBE project. It may be helpful to figure out which member of the executive team should reach out to those who may be barriers to help bring these individuals on board.

Board engagement. Depending on the chosen CBE model, the institution's board may need to be briefed. The higher the level of disruption to your institution's status quo, the greater the need for board engagement. As part of ongoing board development, presidents typically share innovations and new approaches in higher education. A strategy should be created to increase your board's familiarity with CBE and your institution's desire to be part of this national movement. You can anticipate that board members will ask common questions such as the following:

- What is CBE?
- What makes CBE different from traditional offerings?
- Why is it worth investing the institution's human and financial resources in CBE?
- How does this type of program serve today's higher education learner?
- Would we offer the same academic program in traditional and CBE formats?
- Will this expand the total number of learners or take the same learners and move them from a traditional format to CBE?

By educating and engaging the board members, you can seek their support in myriad ways. On the basis of the composition of your board, these individuals could be leveraged to determine the most pressing workforce needs, validate competency sets, and connect program developers with subject matter experts. In addition, board members could provide seed money to help with needed resources.

Communicating the vision. The CBE vision needs to be shared not only with the board but also with faculty, staff, and administration. To help gain a broad base of support from the university community, the executive team should express its unequivocal support for CBE and the program's leadership. This message should be repeated frequently so individuals are assured of the institution's commitment to CBE. It is important to paint the big picture for CBE, even if the institution will be starting with a scaled-down model. Seeing the desired result, individuals can envision a place where they can contribute their talents and expertise. At this point, many institutions find it incredibly helpful to engage external CBE experts during this process. By conducting workshops and presentations, external experts can validate and lend credibility to the big picture vision and share where your institution fits within the national landscape.

Step 2: Development Team Is Established

Now that the executive team has created and communicated the CBE vision, a development team needs to be formed to move the institution from vision to reality.

Selecting a champion. Every CBE program needs to have a champion, the one person responsible for and accountable to the executive team on the program's development. It may be that you will serve as the champion because you have taken the time to read this book and better understand CBE. It may be that you will find someone else to lead this effort. The CBE champion should be someone who has influence and connections on campus and in the broader community. This person needs to have a great number of competencies, including the following:

- Be knowledgeable of CBE.
- Understand the national movement and the institution's place in the movement.
- Be able to persevere, even when facing significant resistance.
- Be able to drive results, staying focused on the desired end result.
- Be able to inspire and motivate others.

- Be able to lead cross-functional teams.
- Be able to effectively communicate with diverse audiences.
- Be able to coordinate different people and processes involved in the build-out.

The CBE champion should have positional authority within the institution. As the level of disruption to the status quo increases, so too does the need to have a champion with positional authority. Regardless, the champion must possess the ability to influence others toward action.

Sole champion caution. This generation of CBE innovators has shared many common challenges, including how CBE champions have come and gone, often leaving their institutions without a champion. Because so few individuals in higher education have CBE expertise and so many institutions are seeking to build programs, some champions have gone on to other institutions, being recruited away because they were recognized for their talents. Other champions were entrepreneurs at heart, and once their programs were built, they moved on to the next innovation in higher education. Others reported having "cashed in" all of their political capital to get the program started and being unable to lead the program long term. The executive team needs to make sure that the champion is surrounded by many people who could step in if the champion were to make an unexpected departure. In addition, executive teams should make clear that CBE is an institutional priority and not just a "pet project" of the CBE champion. For a CBE program's development to be successful, it needs to be not only one person's passion but also a reflection of deeper commitment by the institution. To protect against losing your CBE champion, you need to surround the champion with the resources needed and ensure that individual has access to support and does not feel isolated or left alone. Being a CBE champion is an incredibly challenging position to be in, and these individuals need encouragement and support, including connections with champions at other institutions.

Setting a bigger, broader table. Typically, when those in academia create a new program, the design and development of the program is able to happen within the academic unit. Because

CBE programs often create the need for new processes and systems, faculty cannot create these programs in isolation but must involve the vast majority of nonacademic departments on campus.

CBE programs must establish a cross-functional team, composed of a wide range of competent individuals from multiple areas on campus. Besides being individuals who are able to work on a team, they must be willing to act based on the common good (building the CBE program) and not individual or departmental needs and desires (see Table 8.1).

Hiring staff where expertise is needed. Many programs find that designing, developing, and implementing CBE programs requires hiring additional staff with a different set of skills. Some of these positions may include those listed in Table 8.2.

Training and development for executive and development teams. The executive and development teams need to receive training and development on CBE. This could be done through participation at the Competency-Based Education Network's (C-BEN's) CBExchange, the only all-CBE conference in the United States (see www.cbexchange.org for more information). A host of vendors offer seminars on CBE, including Pearson, Blackboard, D2L, and others. Many higher education associations like the Council for Adult and Experiential Learning (CAEL), EDUCAUSE, the University Professional and Continuing Education Association (UPCEA), and others offer CBE-related sessions at their annual conferences and meetings.

It is advisable for the project champion and development team to scan the resources listed in this book's references. Because this book was designed to generate a high-level understanding of CBE, many of these materials yield a deeper level of knowledge on specific topics. The *Journal of Competency-Based Education*, published by Western Governors University and John Wiley & Sons, is a peer-reviewed, online publication designed to be a primary source of information on CBE (see www.wgu.edu/about_WGU/competency_based_education_journal). This publication features many helpful articles and studies that connect learning sciences with the CBE pedagogy.

Another helpful resource is C-BEN's CBE Design Planner (see www.cbedesignplanner.org). Working together, C-BEN institutions created this interactive tool to help institutions get started

TABLE 8.1

Functional Area for Inclusion and Sample of Competencies Needed

Functional Area for Inclusion	Sample of Competencies Needed
Financial aid: It is absolutely essential to include financial aid in the design process if designing a direct assessment program or if time is flexible.	Individuals need to deeply understand financial aid regulations, be able to think creatively about how to comply with regulations, and be able to tolerate risk.
Business office: Since many CBE programs use different pricing methods, including subscription model pricing, it will be important to bring the business office team into the conversation early.	Individuals need to be able to identify a new or modified business model and design and implement new policies, procedures, and processes to support the model.
Registrar's office: The registrar's office is absolutely essential regardless of the chosen competency-based education (CBE) model. Because CBE programs look to use a competency-based transcript, modifications in this area will be needed.	Individuals must know the institution's policies and procedures related to articulating and transcripting learning and transferring learning to and from the institution, be able to tolerate risk and uncertainty, and have an innovative spirit and a willingness to try new and emerging methods.
Information technology: Information technology is absolutely essential regardless of the chosen CBE model. Typically, CBE programs require different or modified technology solutions.	Individuals know the systems currently used by the institution, including contract terms; stay connected with other vendors and advancements in the IT higher education field; are able to think creatively about solutions; and desire to find automated solutions to manual processes and systems.
Admission and recruiting: These are absolutely essential regardless of the chosen CBE model, because recruiting students is core to all programs.	Individuals have knowledge of the needs and wants of the CBE program's target audience, are able to design a recruitment strategy to reach the target audience, and are able to be the voice of learners in many conversations.

(*Continues*)

TABLE 8.1 (*Continued*)

Functional Area for Inclusion	Sample of Competencies Needed
Faculty senate and governance: On the basis of the level of disruption and your institution's structure, representatives from this area may be needed to represent the faculty voice in any potential redesign of the faculty role.	Individuals have knowledge of faculty policies and procedures, including union rules if applicable, and are able to think creatively about the role of faculty in today's technology-enabled learning environment.
General education committee: This committee is absolutely essential if the chosen CBE model seeks to offer general education courses using CBE pedagogy.	Individuals have knowledge of the general education program, course content, and established learning outcomes; have familiarity with the faculty teaching courses in the general education program; and have demonstrated capacity to think creatively about general education learning outcomes.
Institutional research: This is absolutely essential regardless of the chosen CBE model, because best practice requires evidence-driven design and continuous improvement processes.	Individuals are familiar with institutional-, program-, and course-level data collection and analysis and are able to articulate and design an evidence-based data collection process.
Other academic leaders: On the basis of the intended scope and impact of CBE, additional academic leaders (e.g., deans, division chairs) may need to be involved for establishing competency definitions, mastery definitions, and the like.	Individuals comprehensively understand the courses and content composing their academic program, are able to articulate crosscutting competencies, and have demonstrated the capacity for working collaboratively outside their academic area.

TABLE 8.2
Typical Positions Needed and Primary Competencies

Typical Position Needed	Primary Competencies
Instructional designer	Individuals possess subject matter expertise in instructional theory and are able to create, design, and suggest learning activities and experiences that will help learners acquire necessary competencies.
Curriculum designer	Individuals have knowledge in creating a stimulating and engaging learning journey; are able to evaluate how well the learning journey yields competent learners; are able to knit together often disparate content into an organized, coherent curriculum; and are skilled in creating and refining curriculum maps and leading faculty through the development process.
Psychometrician or assessment designer	Individuals have knowledge of a variety of assessment methods, including which tools should be used and when; are able to establish the reliability and validity of selected tools; are able to write and interpret a range of assessments; and provide evidence-driven research to support curricular modifications based on learner performance.
Recruiter	Individuals have knowledge of the target audience, are able to connect with and market to the program's target audience, create and implement marketing efforts, and are able to establish a network of connections to potential students.
Success coach	Individuals are able to help individuals determine, set, and achieve personal and professional goals; are natural encouragers and motivators; are able to establish rapport and relationships with diverse student populations; and are able to offer a personalized approach to service delivery.

in the CBE design process. It is organized around the quality elements of CBE programs, and leaders can read about the variety of models by element. By selecting their preferred model variation, leaders are provided a list of questions to be answered as a jumping-off point. This resource can be an invaluable resource for institutions.

C-BEN's website (see www.cbenetwork.org) also features a host of resources that beginning institutions benefit from reviewing. For example, the resource guides for financial aid professionals and information technology professionals are worth distribution to your development team (see www.cbenetwork .org/resource-library/). CAEL, EDUCAUSE, and others have produced resources as well and merit your review.

Step 3: Begin the CBE Development Process

As the development team begins its work in program design, the executive team should do its best to empower the development team. Providing guidance on the decision-making process and establishing a timeline for completion can be extremely helpful in setting this team up for success.

Establish the decision-making process. The executive team should decide on and clearly articulate to others the decision-making process. Executives should determine if the development team has the authority to make binding decisions or if it is just making recommendations and providing rationale for its recommendations to the executive team who will then make the ultimate decisions. Furthermore, by looking at the list of decisions that need to be made, the executive team should determine which decisions they would like to make and which ones can be delegated to the development team. When possible, it is beneficial for the executive team to indicate which questions need to have more than internal input. Providing the development team members with guidance on whom they should ask externally for assistance is most helpful.

Set a realistic but motivating timeline. Institutions can build programs in as little as six months with intense effort and resources. Other institutions take a much longer time to build their programs, often over a course of two to three years. When looking at the tasks to be completed, the executive team should set a realistic but motivating timeline. By keeping some level of time-based pressure on the development team, the executive team can help ensure that the project is less likely to stall or its leaders won't lose motivation.

Determine the communication process. As multiple people begin working on different components of the design process, it is essential to have a solid communication process in place. This process should clearly outline protocols and professional behavior expectations. For example, if you commit to provide information by a certain date, what will happen if someone misses a deadline? You should determine the best methods for communication with the group. Either in discussions with the development team or with the guidance of the executive team, the champion should determine answers to these questions:

- Will there be in-person meetings or just electronic communication?
- How frequently will the full development team meet?
- Will sub-team meetings be needed? If so, how often?
- How can information be best conveyed?
- Do you need a virtual workspace?
- Can you manage through other means, such as Google Drive?
- How do you keep people engaged and on the same page?

It is essential for the CBE champion to establish and publish team expectations so all members know what is required of them. Behaviors that deviate from expectations should be addressed quickly with poor performers so the team maintains its vitality and effectiveness.

Start answering design questions. Although getting started in the actual design process can seem overwhelming, breaking down the tasks into pieces is a helpful starting point. Institutions often get started by creating a list of questions they must answer. You could generate your own list of questions or use C-BEN resources, such as the CBE Design Planner, for a prepared list of questions to be answered. The following is a starting list of important questions for the development team to answer:

- How does your institution define *competency-based education* or *competency-based learning*?
- How will you define a competency?
- How will you define or determine mastery?
- What program or programs will you offer?
- Who is your target population?
- What is your delivery modality?
- What technology systems will you use?
- What will your business model be?
- What faculty model will you use?
- What student support services will you offer?
- What policies and procedures will need to change to accommodate your CBE program?
- Will you be a course-based, credit-hour program or a direct assessment program?
- What are your regional accreditors' guidelines for approval?
- Will you build your program from the ground up, deconstruct and reconstruct an existing program, or use a competency framework?
- How, if at all, will you allow for prior learning assessment?
- Will you accept financial aid?
- How will you determine and validate competencies?
- How will learning be transferred into and out of your institution from other institutions and settings?
- What type of transcription will you use?
- How will you train and develop faculty and staff?

Group tasks by category and assign leads. If possible, group tasks into common groups. For example, tasks related to technology (e.g., determining if the current technology can support the CBE program, contacting current and prospective vendors about CBE solutions, evaluating contract terms with current vendors) can be grouped together and assigned to a subcommittee. By assigning a lead and a small team for each subcommittee, you can maximize the amount of progress made over a given period of time, because groups are working on different issues simultaneously. An added benefit is that the CBE champion can work with subcommittee leads, reducing the number of individuals to be managed, as leads should be held accountable for making sure progress is being made. Also, leads will be responsible for engaging the right internal and external subject matter experts as their subcommittee makes key decisions and recommendations. The executive team and CBE champion should consider if a member of the executive committee should serve on each subcommittee or if these groups are able to work more independently.

Keep a running list of outstanding items. As the executive team, development team, and subcommittees perform their work, they will generate tasks for other groups to determine. For example, the technology group may determine that they need to acquire a new learning management platform. This will require instructional designers and faculty to be trained on a new platform. This task (to be trained on the platform) is added to a running list of outstanding items. When the next development team meeting occurs, all outstanding items are discussed and assigned to the proper subcommittee for handling.

Conclusion

By following the guidance offered in this book, you should find that starting your own CBE program should be a much easier process. For us, the book's authors, there was no guidebook to CBE, as we each built our own CBE models. We learned many lessons the hard way, and we hope sharing our learning with you will be beneficial and keep you from making some of our mistakes. Prior to starting our own CBE programs, we did not know one another. Yet, individually, we recognized the need to be connected with others who were trying to do something similar on their own campuses. C-BEN brought us together so we could collectively solve the challenges facing institutions seeking to build and scale high-quality CBE programs. Just five years after C-BEN brought us all together, we stay in regular communication with each other and continue our commitment to removing barriers, building capacity, and growing demand for CBE programmatic offerings.

We encourage you to connect with others in the field and to resist building a program in isolation from your higher education colleagues. By working alongside others, you can find your place in the national movement and help to position your institution as a leader in this space. In addition, we hope you will share your hits and misses with others so the field can learn from you and your experience. Together we can harness the potential of the CBE ecosystem and promote and advance CBE as a strong and legitimate pathway to high-quality degrees and credentials for all learners.

REFERENCES

2015 training industry report. (2015, November/December). *Training Magazine*. Retrieved from https://trainingmag.com/trgmag-article/2o15-training-industry-report

Abel, N. (2016, February 17). What is personalized learning? *International Association for K–12 Online Learning*. Retrieved from http://www.inacol.org/news/what-is-personalized-learning/

Adelman, C., Ewell, P., Gaston, P., & Schneider, C. G. (2014). *The Degree Qualifications Profile: A learning-centered framework for what college graduates should know and be able to do to earn the associate, bachelor's or master's degree.* Lumina Foundation. Retrieved from https://www.luminafoundation.org/files/resources/dqp.pdf

Association of American Colleges & Universities. (2018). *About LEAP*. Retrieved from https://www.aacu.org/leap

Astin, A. W., Banta, T. W., Cross, K. P., El-Khawas, E., Ewell, P. T., Hutchings, P., . . . Wright, B. D. (1992). *Principles of good practice for assessing student learning.* American Association for Higher Education. Retrieved from http://www.learningoutcomesassessment.org/PrinciplesofAssessment.html

Baker, R. B. (2015). *The student experience: How competency-based education providers serve students.* Center on Higher Education Reform: American Enterprise Institute. Retrieved from https://www.luminafoundation.org/files/resources/the-student-experience.pdf

Bergeron, D. (2013, March). *Applying for Title IV eligibility for direct assessment (competency-based) programs* [Dear Colleague letters]. Retrieved from https://ifap.ed.gov/dpcletters/GEN1310.html

Carnegie Foundation for the Advancement of Teaching. (1906). *Annual report: Carnegie Foundation for the Advancement of Teaching.* Retrieved from https://archive.org/details/annualrepor1905a06carnuoft

Carnevale, A. P., Smith, N., & Strohl, J. (2013, June 26). *Recovery: Job growth and education requirements through 2020.* Georgetown University, Center on Education and the Workforce. Retrieved from https://cew.georgetown.edu/cew-reports/recovery-job-growth-and-education-requirements-through-2020/

Christenson, C. (2011). *The innovator's dilemma.* New York, NY: Harper Business Essentials.

Cleary, M. N., Davis, V., Evans, J., Franklin, J., Humphreys, D., Jones, K., . . . Sneath, W. (2015, December). *Faculty and staff roles and responsibilities in the design and delivery of competency-based programs: A C-BEN snapshot.* Competency-Based Education Network. Retrieved from http://www.cbenetwork.org/resource-library/?category=141246

Competency-Based Education Network. (2015). *First year: Discoveries and findings.* Retrieved from http://www.cbenetwork.org/sites/457/uploaded/files/CBENFirstYearReport.pdf

Competency-Based Education Network. (2016, October). *Workbook from CBExchange 2016: Listening, learning and leading.* Phoenix, AZ.

Competency-Based Education Network. (2017a, May). *Quality Framework for Competency-Based Education Programs.* Retrieved from http://www.cbenetwork.org/sites/457/uploaded/files/CBE17__Quality_Standards_FINAL.pdf

Competency-Based Education Network. (2017b, September). *Quality framework for competency-based education programs.* Retrieved from http://www.cbenetwork.org/sites/457/uploaded/files/CBE_Quality_Framework.pdf

Council for Adult and Experiential Learning. (2015). *City University of Seattle (CityU): Performance-based degree model—A competency-based education case study.* Retrieved from http://www.cael.org/cbe/publication/city-of-seattle-cityu-performance-based-degree-model

Council of Regional Accrediting Commissions. (2015, June 2). *Regional accreditors announce common framework for defining and approving competency-based education programs* [Joint statement]. Retrieved from http://download.hlcommission.org/C-RAC_CBE_Statement_6_2_2015.pdf

Craig, R. (2016, November 3). Tuition assistance programs: The secret employee benefit. *Forbes.* Retrieved from https://www.forbes.com/sites/ryancraig/2016/11/03/tuition-assistance-programs-the-secret-employee-benefit/#287588e542cf

Credential Registry. (2017). *Credential engine technical planning.* Retrieved from https://www.credentialengine.org/credentialregistry

Desrochers, D. M., & Staisloff, R. L. (2016, October). *Competency-based education: A study of four new models and their implications for bending the higher education cost curve.* rpk Group. Retrieved from https://www.luminafoundation.org/files/resources/cbe-study-of-4-models.pdf

EDUCAUSE. (2005). *Potential learning activities.* Retrieved from http://net.educause.edu/upload/presentations/NLII052/GS08/learning%20activities%20v5%201.pdf

Everhart, D., Sandeen, C., Seymour, D., & Yoshino, K. (2014). *Clarifying competency based education terms*. American Council on Education, and Blackboard. Retrieved from http://images.email .blackboard.com/Web/BlackboardInc/%7B2a4b9de0-d95f-4159-98a2-b5b305affdcc%7D_Clarifying_CBE_Terms.pdf

Fain, P. (2015a, October). Caution on competency. *Inside Higher Ed.* Retrieved from https://www.insidehighered.com/news/2015/10/05/us-inspector-general-criticizes-accreditor-over-competency-based-education

Fain, P. (2015b, September). Keeping up with competency. *Inside Higher Ed.* Retrieved from https://www.insidehighered.com/news/2015/09/10/amid-competency-based-education-boom-meeting-help-colleges-do-it-right

Fain, P. (2016, January). The faculty role online, scrutinized. *Inside Higher Ed.* Retrieved from https://www.insidehighered.com/news/2016/01/15/education-departments-inspector-generals-high-stakes-audit-western-governors-u

Federal Student Aid. (2017, December 14). *Experiments*. Retrieved from https://experimentalsites.ed.gov/exp/approved.html

Fleming, B. (2014, November 4). Insights on competency-based education: The view from the 20th annual Online Learning Consortium Annual Conference. EDUVENTURES. Retrieved from http://www.eduventures.com/2014/11/insights-competency-based-education-view-20th-annual-online-learning-consortium-international-conference/

Garrett, R., & Lurie, H. (2016). *Deconstructing CBE: An assessment of institutional activity, goals, and challenges in higher education*. Retrieved from http://www.eduventures.com/2016/07/deconstructing-cbe-eduventures-and-ellucian-team-up/

Goodman, M. J., Sands, A. M., & Coley, R. J. (2015, January). *America's skills challenge: Millennials and the future*. Educational Testing Service. Retrieved from https://www.ets.org/s/research/30079/asc-millennials-and-the-future.pdf

Heick, T. (2014, June 16). The characteristics of a highly effective learning environment. TeachThought. Retrieved from http://www .teachthought.com/learning/10-characteristics-of-a-highly-effective-learning-environment/

Hope, J. (2015, March 16). Be ready for the challenges of competency-based programs. *The Successful Registrar*, *15*(2), 1–7. doi:10.1002/tsr.30045

Immerwahr, J., Johnson, J., & Gasbarra, P. (2008, October). *The Iron Triangle: College presidents talk about costs, access, and quality*. The National Center for Public Policy and Higher Education and Public Agenda. Retrieved from http://www.highereducation.org/reports/iron_triangle/IronTriangle.pdf

Kanter, M., Ochoa, E., Nassif, R., & Chong, F. (2011, July 21). *Meeting President Obama's 2020 college completion goal.* Retrieved from https://www.ed.gov/news/speeches/meeting-president-obamas-2020-college-completion-goal

Kotter, J. P. (2012). *Leading change.* Boston, MA: Harvard Business Review Press.

Kotter, J. P. (2014). *XLR8.* Boston, MA: Harvard Business Review Press.

Laitinen, A. (2012, September 5). *Cracking the credit hour.* New America Foundation and Education Sector. Retrieved from https://www.newamerica.org/education-policy/policy-papers/cracking-the-credit-hour/

Leuba, M. (2015, October 12). Competency-based education: Technology challenges and opportunities. *EDUCAUSE Review.* Retrieved from http://er.educause.edu/articles/2015/10/competency-based-education-technology-challenges-and-opportunities

Leuba, M. (2016, February 22). An evolving technology landscape for competency-based education. *EDUCAUSE Review.* Retrieved from http://er.educause.edu/articles/2016/2/an-evolving-technology-landscape-for-competency-based-education

Lumina Foundation. (2017a). *Facts and figures.* Retrieved from https://www.luminafoundation.org/facts-and-figures

Lumina Foundation. (2017b). *Strategic plan for 2017 to 2020.* Retrieved from https://www.luminafoundation.org/files/resources/strategic-plan-2017-to-2020-apr17.pdf

Lumina Foundation. (2017c). *A stronger nation: Learning beyond high school builds American talent.* Retrieved from http://strongernation.luminafoundation.org/report/2017/#nation

Maki, P. L. (2010). *Assessing for learning: Building a sustainable commitment across the institution* (2nd ed.). Sterling, VA: Stylus.

McTighe, J., & Wiggins, G. (2012). *Understanding by Design framework.* Association for Supervision and Curriculum Development. Retrieved from http://www.ascd.org/ASCD/pdf/siteASCD/publications/UbD_WhitePaper0312.pdf

Merisotis, J. (2015a). *America needs talent.* New York, NY: Rosetta Books.

Merisotis, J. P. (2015b, January 8). Higher education must change to reflect shifting student demographics. *The Hill.* Retrieved from http://thehill.com/blogs/congress-blog/education/228795-higher-education-must-change-to-reflect-shifting-student

My College Guide. (2016). *Competency-based degree program.* Retrieved from http://mycollegeguide.org/college-credit-for-life-experience/competency-degree-programs

Northern Essex Community College. (2017). *FAQs for competency-based education.* Retrieved from http://www.necc.mass.edu/academics/competency-based-education/faqs-for-competency-based-education/

Obama, B. (2009, February 24). *Remarks of President Barack Obama: Address to joint session of Congress* [Transcript]. Retrieved from https://obamawhitehouse.archives.gov/the-press-office/remarks-president-barack-obama-address-joint-session-congress

Olson, R., & Klein-Collins, R. (2015). *Competency-based bachelor of business administration at Brandman University: A competency-based education case study.* Council for Adult and Experiential Learning. Retrieved from http://www.cael.org/cbe/publication/competency-based-bachelor-of-business-administration-at-brandman-university

Organisation for Economic Co-operation and Development. (2014). *Education at a glance 2014: OECD indicators.* Retrieved from http://www.oecd.org/edu/United%20States-EAG2014-Country-Note.pdf

Parsons, K., Mason, D., & Soldner, M. (2016, October). *On the path to success: Early evidence about the efficacy of postsecondary competency-based education programs.* American Institutes for Research. Retrieved from http://www.air.org/resource/path-success-early-evidence-about-efficacy-postsecondary-competency-based-education

PayScale and Future Workplace. (2016). *Leveling up: How to win in the skills economy (2016 workforce-skills preparedness report).* Retrieved from http://www.payscale.com/data-packages/job-skills

Public Agenda. (2015). *Shared design elements and emerging practices of competence-based education programs.* Retrieved from http://www.cbenetwork.org/sites/457/uploaded/files/Shared_Design_Elements_Notebook.pdf

Queen's University. (2011). *Quality assurance agency for higher education.* Retrieved from http://www.qub.ac.uk/directorates/AcademicStudentAffairs/CentreforEducationalDevelopment/AssessmentFeedback/UniversityAssessmentPolicy/

Rick, T. (2014, June 11). Organizational culture eats strategy for breakfast, lunch, and dinner. *Meliorate.* Retrieved from https://www.torbenrick.eu/blog/culture/organisational-culture-eats-strategy-for-breakfast-lunch-and-dinner/

Rizkalla, E. (2016, June 22). Why corporate culture eats strategy for breakfast. *The Huffington Post.* Retrieved from http://www.huffingtonpost.com/emad-rizkalla/why-corporate-culture-eat_b_10573092.html

Seifert, C., & Chapman, R. (2015). The coaching transformation. *Inside Higher Ed.* Retrieved from https://www.insidehighered.com/views/2015/04/27/essay-making-switch-professor-coach

Selingo, J. J. (2015). A new measure for collegiate learning: What presidents think of the promises and pitfalls of competency-based education. *The Chronicle of Higher Education.* Retrieved from http:// images.results.chronicle.com/Web/TheChronicleofHigherEduca tion/%7Ba3f84b2d-ea5d-4be3-bd8c-c7ac9b00c4b9%7D_CBE_ Survey_v7_Interactive.pdf

Shapiro, D., Dundar, A., Huie, F., Wakhungu, P., Yuan, X., Nathan, A., & Hwang, Y. A. (2017, April). *Completing college: A national view of student attainment rates by race and ethnicity—Fall 2010 cohort* (Signature Report No. 12b). Herndon, VA: National Student Clearing House Research Center. Retrieved from https://nscresearchcenter .org/wp-content/uploads/Signature12-RaceEthnicity.pdf

Solér, M. (2016). *Competency-based education model benefits faculty as well as students.* EvoLLLution: A Destiny Solutions Illumination. Retrieved from https://evolllution.com/programming/applied-and-experiential-learning/competency-based-education-models-benefits-faculty-as-well-as-students/

Strausheim, C. (2016, February). Transcript of tomorrow. *Inside Higher Ed.* Retrieved from https://www.insidehighered.com/news/2016/02/29/u-maryland-university-colleges-extended-transcript-new-type-student-record

Suskie, L. (2015). *Five dimensions of quality: A common sense guide to accreditation and accountability.* San Francisco, CA: Jossey-Bass.

The Unique History of WGU. (2017). Western Governors University. Retrieved from https://www.wgu.edu/about_WGU/WGU_story#

U.S. Department of Education. (2013, March 19). *Dear Colleague letter: Applying for Title IV eligibility for direct assessment (competency-based) programs.* Retrieved from https://ifap.ed.gov/dpcletters/GEN1310 .html

U.S. Department of Education. (2014, December 19). *Dear Colleague letter: Competency-based education programs—Questions and answers.* Retrieved from https://ifap.ed.gov/dpcletters/GEN1423.html

U.S. Department of Education. (2016, August). *Competency-based education reference guide.* Retrieved from https://experimentalsites .ed.gov/exp/pdf/CBEGuideComplete.pdf

U.S. Department of Education. (2017, September). *Federal student aid handbook.* Retrieved from https://ifap.ed.gov/fsahandbook/ 1718FSAHbkVol3.html

Ward, D. (2013). Sustaining strategic transitions in higher education. *EDUCAUSE Review, 48*(4), 13–22.

Western Governors University. (2016). *Annual report 2016.* Retrieved from https://en.calameo.com/read/00235590470b262a03581

What is competency-based education? (2015). Competency-Based Education Network. Retrieved from http://www.cbenetwork.org/competency-based-education/

ABOUT THE AUTHORS

Deborah J. Bushway currently serves as the provost at Northwest Health Sciences University and as an educational consultant. She has served in a variety of roles prior to this, including senior adviser in the Office of the Undersecretary at the U.S. Department of Education in Washington, DC, interim associate dean at the University of Wisconsin–Extension, and the chief academic officer and vice president of academic innovation at Capella University.

Laurie Dodge currently serves as the vice chancellor for institutional assessment and planning and vice provost at Brandman University. Dodge currently serves as the founding president of the board of directors of the Competency-Based Education Network (C-BEN). She has worked in higher education for over 20 years as a faculty member, interim vice-chancellor of academic affairs, and assessment director. In 2016, she was named one of the "The Sixteen Most Innovative People in Higher Education" by *Washington Monthly*.

Charla S. Long currently serves as executive director of the Competency-Based Education Network, and president of Go Long Consulting. Long was the founding dean of the College of Professional Studies at Lipscomb University and the creator of their nationally acclaimed competency-based education (CBE) model and badging ecosystem. In 2016, Long was recognized by *The Chronicle of Higher Education* as one of the Top 10 Most Influential People in Higher Education for her work in competency-based education.

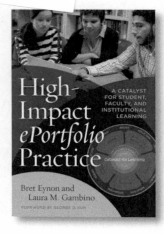

High-Impact ePortfolio Practice
High-Impact ePortfolio Practice

Bret Eynon, and Laura M. Gambino

Foreword by George D. Kuh

"Challenging the noisy legion of digital gurus who see job-specific training as the best choice for first-generation learners, Eynon and Gambino provide compelling evidence that ePortfolios can help underserved students achieve those distinctively twenty-first century liberal arts: agency as motivated learners, creativity in connecting myriad kinds of formal and informal learning, and reflective judgment about their own roles in building solutions for the future. An invaluable resource for all." —*Carol Geary Schneider, Fellow, Lumina Foundation; President Emerita, Association of American Colleges and Universities*

At a moment when over half of US colleges are employing ePortfolios, the time is ripe to develop their full potential to advance integrative learning and broad institutional change. Eynon and Gambino outline how to deploy the ePortfolio as a high-impact practice and describe widely-applicable models of effective ePortfolio pedagogy and implementation that demonstrably improve student learning across multiple settings.

22883 Quicksilver Drive
Sterling, VA 20166-2019

Subscribe to our e-mail alerts: www.Styluspub.com